IS ANY ONE OF YOU SICK?

The biblical basis for healing the sick

Dilwyn Price

Mentor

© Christian Focus Publications
ISBN 185792 242 5
Published in 1997 in the Mentor imprint by Christian Focus Publications,
Geanies House, Fearn, Ross-shire, IV20 1TW, Great Britain

Cover design by Donna Macleod

Printed and bound by J. W. Arrowsmith Ltd, Bristol

Contents

Bible Versions

KJAV The King James or Authorised Version
RSV   The Revised Standard Version 1946
NEB   The New English Bible 1970
Living The Living Bible 1971
GNB   Good News Bible 1976
NIV   The New International Version 1984
NKJV New King James Version 1982
NJB   New Jerusalem Bible 1985
NRSV New Revised Standard Version 1989
REB   Revised English Bible 1989
NCV   New Century Version 1993
CEV   The Promise. Contemporary English Version 1995

Bible quotations are from the New International Version, unless otherwise stated.

The information from C. Rawcliffe is by kind permission of the author.

Acknowledgements

I want to thank my wife, Pam, and family for their love, care and concern. I want to thank the then minister, Rev. Bryan McNeil, deacons and members of Blackhill Baptist Church for their love and prayers. Thank you also to my surgeon, physicians and nurses for caring for me so well and thank you to my partners and staff for putting up with me. I also want to thank my patients for their cards and also prayers in many cases. I know many other Christians have prayed for me. The members of Dundee University Christian Union and the minister, Rev. J. Clark, and members of Central Baptist Church, Dundee were especially kind to my daughter Anna at the time of my illness. I am very grateful to Rev. Martin Graham for his friendship, pastoral care and valued advice in the writing of this book. He and his wife, Phyllis, have been loving and concerned. Thank you to my friend, Mrs. Kath Reed and Pam for reading the script. Although Martin, Kath and Pam have corrected many errors, I take full responsibility for any that are left.

Dr Patrick Dixon gave some valued advice for chapter 12 which I have accepted. I am grateful to him. I must also thank the anonymous reviewer from the Christian Medical Fellowship who offered kind and constructive criticism at an early stage of the work. Much of this advice I accepted.

INTRODUCTION

At the beginning of 1993, the church I attend decided as a body of believers to think and pray about a ministry of healing. I was glad about this because as a General Medical Practitioner, I feel there should be an organised role for the church in praying for the sick. The norm should be when significant illness strikes, that Christians should ask their doctor for help and their church for prayer. I had found, however, that Christian people were strangely reticent about asking for prayer. They were, of course, prayed for when their illnesses became known but this was almost an afterthought with little expectancy.

In February 1993, we had a series of sermons and after church discussions on the subject of healing. We considered especially James chapter 5 as it seemed so clear on the subject. We decided to follow the instructions in that passage.

I had felt that I wanted to write a book or at least some notes on the subject. This was partly to get my own thoughts clear. Another reason was that much I had read in other books did not agree with what I understood from the Bible. Also I could not find a recent book in print by a Christian doctor on what Christians should do about illness. However, I did not write the book as I did not feel qualified to do so.

This remained the situation until the facts came home to me in a totally unexpected way. During the summer of 1993 I became ill. Eventually after denying to myself that I was ill, I was found to have cancer of a kidney. I underwent nephrectomy, or removal of the kidney, in November of that year. I don't know why God allowed this disease but I am sure he loves me. I am also sure that he has said to me to follow the advice in his Word.

While, as I said, I was denying the illness, thinking it was 'flu or even M.E., at least two Christian friends reminded me about James chapter 5. I am grateful to them. When the diagnosis of cancer was made, my wife Pam and I talked and prayed about it and then asked our minister and deacons to come and pray over me. They did and anointed me with oil. Pam and I really felt the love of the local Christians. Also we know that Christians in other parts of the country were also praying. We are deeply grateful to everybody.

Talking about five year survivals of 70 to 90 percent[1] is very personal now! I believe God wants me to write this book and so I pray he will use it. I am involved in what I have written. I have been greatly blessed as I have written the work. I praise God that he has protected me from negative thoughts about the disease. Instead of asking, 'Why me?', I have had the distinct feeling that having shown an interest in healing, God has given me some practical experience! I certainly cannot fault his wisdom that I should be my own experiment. At first I did feel sad and worried but I have also experienced the closeness of my heavenly Father. If I had not been convalescing from surgery, I do not think I would have had the time to write a book. If this book helps only one Christian who is ill, I will be satisfied.

I have now returned to work and a number of funny things have happened to me. It has done me good to laugh! The funniest was one lady who had missed me, as her own doctor. We have a loudspeaker system to call the next patient. She said that when she heard my voice, it was like a voice from heaven. I quickly replied that I was glad it wasn't. She immediately saw the funny side and we laughed together.

One of the things that has encouraged me so much in my illness has been that it has brought me nearer to God. Pam and I have really been aware of his love and concern and this has brought us closer together. We want to praise him. Other people have also commented on this renewed love for God in time of illness (see

---

1. Doctors do not talk about cure of cancer in medical journals because some cancers may return after many years. They talk for example of five year survivals of say 60%. This means that six out of ten people with that disease are alive at five years.

Fear no Evil by David Watson, for example). The Psalms are a good way for expressing these feelings of love to God when we are so overwhelmed with emotion that we do not know what to say:

> Praise the LORD, my soul!
>> All my being, praise his holy name!
> Praise the LORD, my soul,
>> and do not forget how kind he is.
> He forgives all my sins
>> and heals all my diseases....
> The LORD is merciful and loving,
>> slow to become angry and full of constant love.
> He does not keep rebuking;
>> he is not angry for ever.
> He does not punish us as we deserve
>> or repay us according to our sins and wrongs.
> As high as the sky is above the earth,
>> so great is his love for those who honour him.
> As far as the east is from the west,
>> so far does he remove our sins from us.
> As a father is kind to his children,
>> so the LORD is kind to those who honour him.
> He knows what we are made of;
>> he remembers that we are dust...
> But for those who honour the LORD,
>> his love lasts for ever....
>> who faithfully obey his commands.......
> Praise the LORD, my soul!   (Psalm 103, GNB)

Dear Christian friend, if you are suffering or about to undergo major surgery, rest assured that the Lord is with you. Ask the leaders of your church to pray with you.

There is the possibility that you have picked up this book and you do not know Jesus as your Lord and Saviour. You may have looked at it out of curiosity or because you are ill and need help. My great desire and prayer is that you will come to know him, who died in your place for your sins, and knowing him you will have eternal life. Knowing the Lord Jesus Christ personally is far more important than healing of any disease. God in his goodness invites us to call upon him in any time of trouble. He is concerned about us.

Chapter 1

JAMES GIVES HIS ADVICE

This book is an attempt by me as a Christian and practising doctor to understand the biblical teaching on healing. God, in his grace, has given a great deal of knowledge to the medical profession. This is being used by believers and non-believers alike to alleviate suffering and cure diseases. For this we can truly thank our heavenly Father. However, in my work, I find there is so much suffering that medical treatment cannot help and people die despite the best efforts. There are many diseases that cannot be cured, but their symptoms can be eased. An example is rheumatoid arthritis; doctors talk about the management of such a disease, rather than cure. Sometimes pain is caused by our natures, rather than a disease as such; this is the case in many psychological disorders. The Bible talks about healing of diseases, healing of our personalities, indeed healing of body, soul and spirit, whereas doctors very rarely talk about healing, except, perhaps, the healing of wounds. In the example of rheumatoid arthritis, the disease may not be cured but the accompanying sadness, bitterness or fear can often be healed. I believe, therefore, that the church should be more active in this area.

We can thank God that many churches have realised this and pray for the sick, hold healing services and so on. Many marvellous healings have taken place through this work; but many more people have not been healed. When somebody is not healed, this may be attributed to unbelief of the people praying or even unbelief of the sick one. This accusation will cause increased suffering as the sick person and his or her friends desperately try to bolster their faith or seek some hidden sin. The cycle of discovering and confessing sin may be repeated over and over again and yet the illness does not go away. None of us is perfect, so we can always find something to confess. A vicious circle develops where the presumed lack of faith is considered as the sin and then we have difficulty believing that our lack of faith is forgiven. We need to see what the Bible says about these things.

What the Bible says

The clearest teaching and indeed command in the Bible is found in James 5:13-16:

> Is any of you in trouble? He should pray. Is anyone happy? Let him sing songs of praise. Is any one of you sick? He should call the elders of the church to pray over him and anoint him with oil in the name of the Lord. And the prayer offered in faith will make the sick person well; the Lord will raise him up. If he has sinned he will be forgiven. Therefore confess your sins to each other and pray for each other so that you may be healed. The prayer of a righteous man is powerful and effective.

This is a very clear command to the church. If we are in trouble we should pray; if happy we should praise God; and if we are sick, we should ask the church to pray for us. The blessing promised by God in answer to such a prayer offered in faith is tremendous: the sick one will be made well; he will be raised up, presumably from his sick-bed; and his sins, if any, will be forgiven. What a promise! The significant phrase is 'the prayer in faith'. What does it mean? The answer to this question is perhaps the most important part of this book. Chapter 4 is devoted to it.

Over the centuries the church has neglected this passage to her great detriment. Certainly the churches I have been a member of have not emphasised this passage. 'You do not have, because you do not ask God' (James 4:2). I hesitate to say that Christians have suffered more than they should by not asking for this blessing, because our dear heavenly Father loves us so much and nothing can separate us from his love given in our Lord Jesus Christ. However, as a doctor, I have come to realise how lovely it is for believers to share in these things and so comfort a sick person in the name of the Lord. We need to encourage each other to ask for prayer in times of serious illness, remembering that the fittest of us will one day be sick unless the Lord comes first.

Why has the church neglected this blessing and ministry of healing? There are a number of possible reasons.

1. *Christian people have found it not to be true*

I think to be honest with ourselves we have to face this possibility. Believers have, as a church, prayed for their loved ones, pleaded for faith, anointed with oil; and yet those people have died. Think of what it must have been like during the Black Death or bubonic plague in the Middle Ages, for example, or the suffering in the families affected by diphtheria at the turn of the last century. The believers prayed and prayed and still their loved ones died. Perhaps they then became fatalistic, accepting that what will be, will be. In other words there was no point in praying for healing. I think that probably this did happen. The accepted wisdom was the words of Job, 'The LORD gave and the LORD hath taken away; blessed be the name of the LORD' (Job 1:21, AV).

Martin Luther was very critical of the letter of James, he called it 'the epistle of straw'. He said that even if James was to be followed, the practice as followed by the Catholic Church did not work. He wrote 'scarcely 1 in 1000 is restored, and then no one thinks it is by the sacrament, but by the help of nature or medicine'.[1] There is evidence that Luther changed his mind about healing in later life.

I must mention here the comfort that God gives and the assurance that the loved ones are safe in the arms of their Saviour. Believers did and do pray for their sick friends. If they could not be healed, they asked that God would comfort them and receive them into heaven. For the Christian death leads to complete and perfect healing.

This is the glory of true Christianity. 'Who shall separate us from the love of Christ? ... For I am convinced that neither death nor life will be able to separate us...' (Rom. 8:35ff.). 'For the

Lord himself will come down from heaven, and the dead in Christ will rise first. After that, we who are still alive and are left will be caught up with them in the clouds to meet the Lord in the air' (1 Thess. 4:16,17). Praise God.

God, who in Christ died and rose again for us, does not mock us. His Word is true because he says so. James 5 is therefore true. He asks us so to believe, even if at first sight it does not seem to fit in with our experience. I hope to show as I proceed that James' words are true and reliable.

There is some evidence that people did not give up completely during the Black Death. It seems the church applied the quarantine principles detailed in Leviticus chapters 13 to 15 and this gradually controlled the disease. I am sure this was accompanied by much prayer.

2. The church may have adapted the passage

This has in fact happened. The Roman Catholic sacrament of Extreme Unction (or the Last Rites or Anointing) was based upon this passage. It was first mentioned in the eighth century and confirmed by the Council of Trent in the sixteenth century. This anointing was attacked by John Calvin.[2] One of his basic arguments was that the gift of healing had disappeared! He admitted that anointing may have been a sacrament used by the apostles, but not by anybody else. He claimed that the gift of healing was temporary, ceasing partly due to man's ingratitude.

According to the Catholic Church, the sacrament was conferred only on those who were seriously ill, which fits in with James in that the elders (or priests) went to the sick person, not the other way round. It was only to be given once during the illness and was to strengthen both body and soul. Sadly, it gradually was postponed until the person was at death's door, and certainly in the popular mind it had nothing to do with healing but was an essential preparation for eternity, being associated with penitence and death.

Even as late as 1945, Pickar in the Catholic Bulletin Quarterly emphasised Extreme Unction.[3] However, in his 'Is any one sick among you?' he wrote: 'The prayer of faith will save the sick man from physical pains of weakness, sorrow of soul, affliction of mind, fear of death, dread of judgement, horror of punishment, remorse of conscience, diffidence and temptation of despair.' Interestingly, his is the only work that I have found with a title similar to this present book.

The sacrament was re-established as *Sacram unctionem infirmorum* – 'Anointing of the Sick' by Pope Paul VI in 1972 after the Second Vatican Council. This emphasised the prayer for healing: 'May the Lord who frees you from sin save you and raise you up.' A statement issued during the Council in 1963 said that the sacrament was not for those only who were at the point of death but in danger of death, in other words those who are seriously ill.[4] The sacrament could be repeated if the illness became worse or before a serious operation. At the point of death the Catholic priest celebrates communion called the Viaticum which *is* a preparation for eternity.[5]

The Protestant Churches may have neglected James' words because Extreme Unction seemed almost magical and was open to abuse. People like Calvin were so incensed by Extreme Unction at the point of death and the use of oil that had to be blessed by bishops that they 'threw the baby out with the bath water' and neglected the Word of God in James.

3. *Perhaps the letter of James is not for the whole church*

The letter starts, 'James, a servant of God and of the Lord Jesus Christ, to the twelve tribes scattered among the nations: Greetings.' It is generally agreed that this James is the brother of Jesus. He was converted after Jesus' resurrection and became a leader of the church in Jerusalem. It is obvious that he is writing to Christians because of the reference, 'believers in our glorious Lord Jesus Christ' (2:1). Tasker suggested that 'twelve tribes' could mean

Jewish Christians scattered abroad during the persecution after the death of Stephen in Acts 7.[6] The twelve tribes, being the descendants of Abraham who was given the promises, could speak of the true spiritual descendants of Abraham, those who believe in his Seed, the Lord Jesus Christ (Gal. 3:7,16). However, the important point is that there is no difference between Jewish and non-Jewish Christians. We have the same Lord, the same Spirit, same inheritance, same promises, one body – the church, and indeed are all one in Christ Jesus (Rom. 10:12; 1 Cor. 12:13; Gal. 3:28; Eph. 3:6). We can safely accept these words as the Word of God to us.

4. Has Medical Science removed the need of Christian Healing?

Modern medicine can cure diseases like the Black Death, cholera and diphtheria. Public health action has largely prevented the old killers, but they re-appear in times of war and famine. As long as funds are available, the individual can so often be saved by modern techniques.

All knowledge is given by God but, by the very fact that not everybody gets well after medical treatment, this knowledge is imperfect. I strongly believe that if illness strikes, the proper course is to pray, seek medical help and continue to pray. There is then a partnership in healing, even though unbelieving doctors may not realise it!

There has, in fact, been a sad separation between the church and the healing professions. Luke, the doctor, was Paul's dear friend (Col. 4:14). The Book of Ecclesiasticus is not thought by most to be divinely inspired, but it does reflect the views of the Jews a century or so before Christ was born. In Ecclesiasticus 38:1-14 we read:

'Honour the doctor for his services,
for the Lord created him.
His skill comes from the Most High,....
The Lord has imparted knowledge to men,

that by their use of his marvels he may win praise;
by using them the doctor relieves pain....
There is no end to the works of the Lord,
who spreads health over the whole world.

My son, if you have an illness, do not neglect it,
but pray to the Lord, and he will heal you.
Renounce your faults, amend your ways,
and cleanse your heart from all sin.....
Then call in the doctor, for the Lord created him;
do not let him leave you, for you need him.
There may come a time when your recovery is in their hands;
then they too will pray to the Lord
to give them success in relieving pain
and finding a cure to save their patient's life.' (NEB)

There are three points in this passage: (1) The doctor, his skill and the medicines are all from God; (2) Illness may be caused by sin; (3) The doctor should pray for God's help. Apparently in the early centuries of the church, there was a partnership with doctors,[7] presumably associated with miraculous healings in the time of the apostles, at least. However, pagan rites came in and medical care deteriorated to magic. Meanwhile, among Christians, the idea arose of withdrawal from the world, neglect of the body and even buffeting of it into submission. Hermits, with filthy, wasted, lice infested bodies, were considered very holy. Such neglect of biblical instructions for cleanliness paved the way for the great plagues like the Black Death.

There were bright spots in the darkness. Around 250, Dionysius recorded Christians tending the sick who had plague, at great danger to themselves. In 529, Benedict insisted that the care of the sick came before all things.[8] Great hospitals like St. Bartholemew's in London came from this work of the monks and really, it was they who continued basic care of the sick. Scientific medicine eventually got going but by then the split between the care of the sick and the care of the soul was established. Many doctors cannot see the relevance of James 5, because they do not know God. To the Christian doctor, I believe this passage is very relevant as I will try to show.

5. *Gifts of healing have been withdrawn*

There is the possibility that the ministry of healing has been withdrawn by the Holy Spirit: that healing was a special sign only during the time of the apostles; or that it was withdrawn because of the Church's unbelief. John Calvin held both reasons for the lack of healing in his time. He also said that miracles ceased so that the preaching of the gospel would be more glorious. There is, however, nothing in the Bible to suggest that anything the apostles did would cease when they died. Unbelief may have been a cause, but who are we to say? Were the great men and women of God in the past less holy than we are? I doubt it. I believe, however, that the Holy Spirit is making us more aware of these things in our day. So rather than criticising the people of the past, we should consider our own belief and obedience. I mentioned above that Calvin was so thrilled with the preaching of the glorious gospel that he thought that miracles would obscure it. In recent times, the glorious gospel is being made more glorious by the Spirit giving signs and wonders.

6. *James 5 is about spiritual healing only*

It is possible that James 5 is not about physical (or mental) healing at all, but about spiritual healing. Most commentators I have read, state that it is about physical healing. One exception is J.R.Blue.[9] He states that James was writing 'to those who had grown weary, who had become weak both morally and spiritually in the midst of suffering'. His argument is based on the word used for 'sick' in James 5. He does not comment on the Authorised Version's translation – 'and the prayer of faith shall *save* the sick' – rather than *heal* as in other versions. The difficulty in Blue's interpretation is that the meaning would be that the prayer of faith would heal or save from sin. Traditionally the church has always accepted that James meant illness, otherwise how would 'the last rites' have arisen? Calvin[10] in the sixteenth century understood James to mean illness as also did Matthew Henry[11] in the eighteenth. The words used by James will be considered in detail later. Taking the passage as a whole, in any version, the first impression is of physical healing. The whole Book of James is written in a clear and straight-forward way. I am sure he is giving advice on what to do if illness strikes.

7. *Fear of causing additional hurt*

Sadly there are extremes in the healing movement. Some of these have been rightly derided by my non-Christian colleagues in the medical profession. Great claims have been made that have been shown to be false. There has been much hurt. This has produced another reason for not following James' advice: fear. Many Christians have been frightened that if they prayed for the sick who were not healed, then they would be responsible for more pain, disappointment and suffering for the sick. I hope to show that as long as we follow in love the guidance of the Holy Spirit in God's Word, we do not need to be afraid.

I believe that James' words are very relevant to us today, as we try to care for the sick. His instructions are relatively neglected in some circles perhaps because a small group, meeting in the sick room, is not as exciting as a public healing service. Because of this, there is much less risk of costly mistakes in the small group. Is this why God exhorts us to 'send for the elders' rather than organise large meetings? We need now to examine the passage in James in more detail and compare it with other Scriptures to find out how to apply it. With God's help this is what I will try to do in the following pages.

References

1. Luther M., quoted in *The Oil of Gladness*, p. 137, ed. Dudley M. & Rowell G., SPCK, 1993.

2. Calvin J., pp.636, 637, *Institutes of the Christian Religion*, Book 4, chapter 19, sections 18, 19, translated by Henry Beveridge. James Clarke and Co. Ltd., 1962.

3. Pickar C., p.172, *Is Anyone Sick Among you?* Catholic Bulletin Quarterly 7, (1945).

4. *Catechism of the Catholic Church*, part 2, sect. 2, art. 5. The Anointing of the Sick, 1513-1515, Geoffrey Chapman, 1994.

5. Crichton J.D., *Understanding the Sacraments*, Geoffrey Chapman/ Castle Publishers, 1993.

6. Tasker R.V.G., p.39, *The General Epistle of James* (Tyndale New Testament Commentaries), Inter-Varsity Press/Eerdmans, 1956.

7. Watt Sir J., *Healing in History* in *What is wrong with Christian Healing*, The Churches' Council for Health and Healing, 1993.

8. Gunstone J., pp.76, 77, *The Lord is our Healer*, Hodder and Stoughton, 1986.

9. Blue J.R. in '*The Bible Knowledge Commentary*', ed. Walvoord J.F. & Zuck R.B, pp.834, 835, *James*, Victor Books, 1983.

10. Calvin, J. *ibid*.

11. Henry M., p.447, *Matthew Henry's Commentary Acts to Revelation*, ed. Winter D., Hodder and Stoughton, 1975.

Chapter 2

THE SICK PERSON

Is any one of you sick? He should call the elders of the church.

In this chapter I would like to concentrate on the sick person and his illness. First of all, he or she is a believer: this passage is advice to Christians. James advised the sick to call the elders of the church. We do not know whether a physician would have been called as well, but certainly the sick one would have been nursed by somebody. This would have included simple medical care.

James is also speaking to our time, as his letter is part of the Word of God. Nowadays I think we can take it for granted that the doctor has been seen, a diagnosis has been made or tests have been arranged, and the suggestion has been made that it is a serious or at least significant illness. I say this, because if it was a minor condition the sick could pray for themselves and go to other believers for prayer rather than having to ask the elders to come. Serious illness is being considered here. However, as every doctor knows, what may seem serious to one person may not to another, and the elders need to be sensitive to this. In psychological illness what may seem trivial to the strong and well may be devastating to the sufferer and it may have needed great determination for the sufferer to ask for prayer. It is less embarrassing for a depressed person to go to the doctor than to ask the elders to pray. Often, however, a relative or friend will have asked for prayer and the mentally sick person may deny illness or even be angry. These are very special circumstances and need much prayer by the elders and co-operation with the doctor. This type of illness, so called psychotic illness, is further considered in chapter 11.

He knows he is sick

The situation here then is that the person knows that he is sick and has asked for prayer from the church. It is important to emphasise that the sick person himself must do the asking. Deep spiritual things are always personal.

Expanding this, let us suppose someone has just been told he has a cancer which needs major surgery. What emotions does he experience? First of all, I think disbelief or denial, 'it's not real'; then fear, sadness and sometimes anger, 'why me?' The sadness occurs because of the possibility of leaving loved ones, especially where there is a young family; and the anger, if any, is directed to doctors or God or both. Acceptance of the situation is the next step; and to the Christian this is knowing God's love afresh and understanding that everything is according to his will. So by personally asking for prayer, the sick Christian is confirming his dependence on his loving heavenly Father and is well along the road of realising that whatever happens, he is in control. Note that this takes faith, and is all the faith the sick one needs.

Speaking the truth in love

This implies other things. The first is that it is wrong to hide from Christians that they are very ill. When I was a medical student in the late sixties, we learnt by example from our medical teachers that it was best to avoid telling patients the bad news. I cannot actually remember formal teaching or advice on this subject. I can still remember the look on a man's face when a consultant told him unconvincingly that he did not have cancer. The poor man did not believe a word of it! As qualified doctors, we often copped out by telling the relatives. This could backfire! Once I told a man that his wife had inoperable cancer. The day before she had had an exploratory operation and advanced cancer was found. He immediately went up to his wife and bluntly told her that she was going to die! At first I was shocked, but it made it so much easier for me to talk to her.

To be honest, I think the main reason for not telling patients the truth is that the doctor is frightened. He is frightened that if he tells the bad news, he will have to get involved and that is costly. I know from experience that it is costly. Sometimes doctors try to get around the problem by not actually telling the truth but not telling a lie either. This is not the same as revealing the truth gradually as the sick one is able to take it – that is good.

A friend of mine was treating a man with leukaemia. I think most people know that leukaemia is cancer or overgrowth of white blood cells at the expense of the red blood cells. My friend's patient asked what exactly was wrong with him. Taking a deep breath, my friend answered that he was making too many white blood cells. The patient answered, 'Oh thank you, doctor, I was worried I had leukaemia!'

Things have changed now, most people are told the truth. One of the books that helped me so much was *Dying* by Hinton.[1] He showed that contrary to our fears most people were glad that they were told the truth. Obviously, the facts should be told gently and gradually as the patient is given the opportunity to ask.

Denial

Christianity is concerned with telling the truth in love, so it is important to comment on denial. This is where a patient is told unmistakeably the truth about their condition but subsequently denies it. Denial is a very common stage to go through after receiving very bad news. The person does not know that his denial is untrue and it is wrong and harmful to try and persuade him otherwise. It is temporary, and not in itself wrong or harmful but a normal psychological defence reaction. However, the reality of denial does not mean that patients should not be told; it is just that the news is so bad that they cannot take it at first and so deny it. The medical carers, relatives and indeed elders need to recognise this. Such a person will 'know' that he is not seriously ill and therefore may not ask for prayer when plainly he needs prayer.

Love and understanding is what he needs, his acceptance of the facts comes later. Denial is not always present.

So often when I, as a doctor, am talking to relatives they ask that their sick loved one is not told, to try and shield him or her from distress. James shows that to do so would deny a lovely experience of God's love just when he or she needs it. People are not daft. After any temporary stage of denial, they know they are ill. To try to pretend otherwise is cruel and not like Christ. There was a couple, let us call them John and Margaret. John was dying from cancer and Margaret did not want him told what was wrong because she loved him too much to hurt him. John knew he was dying but was frightened to talk about it with Margaret as she always avoided talking about his illness. Such a couple may have been married for 20, 30 or 40 years and never have had a secret from each other; but in their last weeks or months together on earth, they had to keep something from each other.

This is wrong. Two of the great things about Christianity are truth and love or rather truth in love, so sharing each other's burdens. Many couples like John and Margaret have been so relieved when the knowledge has been shared.

Sickness of one hurts the whole family

The second point is that the local church is a family and part of the body of Christ. This means, as Paul writes in 1 Corinthians 12:26, that if one member of the family suffers we all suffer. We are so often private individuals and keep things to ourselves perhaps from pride, or from fear of gossip, or because we do not want to bother others. It was said of the early church, 'see how these Christians love each other'. To love others we must be ready to receive love and concern from others, when we need it. So the sick one should ask for prayer and indeed I think in this passage is commanded to ask for prayer.

Occasions when the sick one may not be able to request prayer

The parents or guardians of very young children and those with
severe learning difficulty will obviously have to do the asking. It
is also right for the relatives of those unconscious or sedated in
intensive therapy units (ITU) to ask for prayer on behalf of their
loved ones. An ITU can be a very intimidating place for lay people
but I think two or three elders should go and pray, having discussed
it with the nurse in charge. An ITU is awe-inspiring place, because
there patients are so often brought back from the jaws of death
through high-tech medicine, but we need to remember that God
has given this knowledge.

Why is he sick? – The cause of disease

In medicine, the cause of disease, or aetiology, is described in
pathological terms. These include infective, genetic, neoplastic
(i.e. cancer) and degenerative (growing old). This does not really
answer why am I ill? Why me and not somebody else? The scientific
answer is because of genes and social circumstances. For science
this is fine but pathology does not tell me what the purpose of my
illness is. Deep down, we all want to know why? In many cases,
it is not possible to know the reason why – presumably we will
find out in heaven. However, there are reasons given in the Bible
and I think it is helpful to consider them:

1. Sickness occurs because our world is not now perfect. It has
   been spoiled by man's rebellion against God and also probably
   by Satan's rebellion. The important passage about this is Romans
   8:19-23: '... For the creation was subjected to frustration ... in
   hope that the creation itself will be liberated from its bondage
   to decay.... We know that the whole creation has been groaning
   as in the pains of childbirth right up to the present time.' In
   other words the whole of creation has been damaged by man's
   rebellion against God and like us is groaning, waiting for the
   future glory. Sin entered into the world and because of this,
   God allowed the natural state of decay – living things grow

old and die; mountains are ground down; and eventually the sun will run out of energy. Sickness and disease is part of this process of decay. This is the main explanation for sickness and accidents. God is working to correct this and one day everything will be put right. 'Glory will be revealed in us. The creation waits in eager expectation for the sons of God to be revealed ... in hope that (it) will be liberated and brought into the glorious freedom of the children of God.'

There is another passage: 'The wolf will live with the lamb ... the calf and the lion and the yearling together and a little child will lead them ... the lion will eat straw like the ox. The infant will play near the hole of the cobra .... They will neither harm nor destroy ... for the earth will be full of the knowledge of the LORD' (Isaiah 11:6-9). This is obviously picture language but gives an idea what the world will be like when Jesus returns.

2. Sickness, disease and injury may be and are so often caused by man. The list is endless: smoking, carelessness, alcohol intoxication, drugs, selfishness and greed (e.g. sexually transmitted diseases and diseases caused by obesity and over-eating), war and famine. When we are tempted to blame God, it is instructive to realise how much suffering in the world could be avoided if we respected our bodies properly and loved others as much as we love ourselves.

3. Sickness may be a punishment sent by God. There are many instances in the Old Testament. Examples are Deuteronomy 32:39, 1 Samuel 2:6,7, and 2 Kings 15:5. Until the Book of Job, the Old Testament was quite clear: for the children of Israel, obedience brought divine favour and blessings including long life, fertility and health, while disobedience brought divine anger, including premature death, infertility and disease.[2]

4. Satan or his evil spirits may cause illness. I don't think this necessarily means someone is demon possessed. I think illness caused by Satan will be no different from any other illness and we may never know the real cause; treatment will be the same.

I certainly don't think common or garden illnesses are below the Devil's dignity! Examples from the Bible are deafness, epilepsy, psychiatric illness and one example, a woman, who was bent double for eighteen years (Luke 13:10-17). We are told that some women were healed of evil spirits and sicknesses (Luke 8:2).

5. Sickness may be a chastisement sent by God to Christians. The Book of Job reminds us not to despise the discipline of God. God inflicts pain, and gives relief; he wounds but also heals (Job 5:17-18). God disciplines those he loves (Rev. 3:19), he does it for our good that we may share his holiness (Heb. 12:10). This discipline may include sickness (1 Cor. 11:32). Acceptance of discipline produces peace (Heb. 12:11).

   This teaching, although true, has been used unthinkingly by some and sick people have been hurt. The last thing I want to do is to cause more pain; so if I have worried you, please turn to chapter 6. Those in positions of authority should remember that to decide the cause of another's illness is fraught with danger. To get it wrong will bring judgement to the accuser – remember the speck and the plank (Matt. 7:1-5) and who can throw the first stone (John 8:7)?

6. Sickness or weakness in Christians may be allowed by God so that we don't rely on our own strength. There are many examples, Spurgeon and Cowper suffered from depression. Paul had his thorn in the flesh. He said when he was weak or ill, then he was strong, because Christ's power was made perfect in his weakness (2 Cor. 12:9).

7. Sickness may occur for the works of God to be displayed in someone's life. This was the case in the man who was blind from birth (John 9:2), and also Lazarus. Jesus said that the purpose of Lazarus' illness was not death but for the glory of God (John 11:4). Some people are miraculously healed from serious or fatal diseases; they receive a gift of healing. It is possible that they developed the disease in order to be healed by the power of God, to build up the church.

8. Suffering, including that caused by sickness, may benefit the church. Paul wrote: 'for the sake of Christ's body, the church, I am completing what still remains for Christ to suffer in my own person' (Col. 1:24, REB). 'For just as the sufferings of Christ flow over into our lives, so also through Christ our comfort overflows' (for your comfort, 2 Cor. 1:5). Experiencing illness allows the comforting of the Lord to be shown in the life of the believer which will then benefit other Christians. This is true, we praise God when we see a person who is full of the joy of the Lord despite great suffering.

9. Sickness in Christians may be allowed in order to demonstrate to the Devil and his evil hosts that even in suffering a human being can love God. Job is the classic example of this (Job 1 and 2). Perhaps we will find out one day that God is even now proclaiming to Satan, 'Have you considered my servant Joni (or your, the reader's, name)? She is blameless and upright, a woman who fears God and shuns evil even though you, Satan, have incited me to allow her to suffer.' What glory will await such a person in heaven! I don't know if this is true, but it did happen to Job, so could happen to us.

I have found it helpful to consider these reasons but we need not worry about the cause. We can be assured that even if Satan is the cause, God is still in control and he loves us.

Some mistakes!

The contemporary explanation for two of the greatest epidemics of disease in Europe, namely the Black Death in the fourteenth century and cholera in the nineteenth century, were very similar. They were acts of God, sent to punish mankind for its sinfulness so that the people would repent and turn away from their sin so avoiding eternal damnation. This is too simplistic a view because so many died during the plague and many were innocent children. During the second main outbreak of plague, a disproportionate number of children died[3] – due to immunity in the adults surviving the first attack – and this was put down to lack of respect for parents! Other supposed causes for judgement were the love of tournaments and licentious behaviour. Unfortunately for the moralists, behaviour was just as hedonistic in the survivors when the plague died down. The explanation why the innocent suffered as much as the guilty was that the plague was a sign of God's mercy and grace, since it prompted men to repent in this life and be spared the pains of hell in the next. The Scots were ridiculed by English clerics because they pleaded with God to be excused this grace! The true cause of the plague was Yersinia Pestis carried by fleas from rats which thrived in the dirt and unsanitary conditions (an example of cause 2 above). These conditions were also the cause of cholera.[4]

There are two extreme views, today, of the reason for sickness; and they have caused a great deal of unnecessary suffering. They are: (1) all sickness is caused by personal sin; and (2) symptoms of sickness are a deceit of the devil.

(1) Sickness may be caused by sin but by no means always, this subject is considered in chapter 6.

(2) The second view is that the symptoms of sickness are a deceit of the devil. Because our sicknesses as well as our sins are dealt with on the cross (Isaiah 53, see my chapter 5), the extreme view has arisen that Christians can be free of all sickness. When symptoms do appear, they should be denied – not even prayed over –because illness cannot occur.

This is a complete falsehood, as examples of sickness in the Bible show. We know, from our experience, that it is not true because Christians die. One man said that it is not necessary for Christians, when their time has come to die, to die of sickness; but to 'fall asleep in Jesus Christ'. A doctor, however, can always find something to write on the death certificate. The telling answer to this, however, is found in Isaiah 53. The very passage that, it is claimed, teaches the cure of all disease! Verse 3 states '(Jesus was) a man of sorrows, and familiar with suffering (acquainted with grief, AV).' In verse 4 we read: 'Surely he took up our

infirmities (he hath borne our griefs, AV) and carried our sorrows.'
'Sorrows' is obviously the same word twice; and 'suffering' and
'infirmities' are translations of the same word, 'grief(s)' in the
Authorised Version. If we claim that verse 4 also means 'he took
up our infirmities and carried our diseases' and it does (Matt.
8:17), we must also accept that our Lord Jesus was 'a man with
disease and pain, and familiar with infirmity, weakness or
suffering' (verse 3). I gather the New Jewish Version has 'a man
of suffering and familiar with disease'. If our Lord Jesus, who
was holy, suffered sickness – I write this very reverently – then
obviously we, his servants, will suffer sickness until we join him
in heaven. It is also very interesting that the Greek word translated
as 'infirmities' in Matthew 8 is *asthenes*[5] which is the word for
'sick' in James 5:14.

What is the sickness?

We have discussed the person and the cause of sickness. What is
sickness? Perhaps some ills are excluded in James' instructions?
I can well imagine a depressed Christian in the depths of his
suffering thinking his sickness is excluded from God's help.

The Greek word translated 'sick' is the word *astheneo* which
means without strength, weakness. It is used for both physical
disease and mental afflictions. James could have used a more
precise term for physical disease but he didn't. Hence he includes
all afflictions which cause weakness. We pride ourselves on
recognising the interactions between the mind and the body, but
James, through the Holy Spirit, was ahead of his time. I have known
people who have taken to their beds and been there for years with
no apparent physical complaint. They had found life too difficult
and the weakness of their minds had produced weakness of the
body. *Astheneo* is used sometimes in English illustrating why
James used it to mean any debilitating illness. There are a lot of
diseases that cause tiredness (or weakness) and there is even an
abbreviation now: TATT (tired all the time). My*asthenia* Gravis
is a rare but serious disease that causes severe muscle weakness.

Neur*asthenia* was a term much used in the past for a condition that sounds very much like our Myalgic Encephalomyelitis (M.E.). M.E., also called post viral fatigue syndrome, is associated with weakness of thought and muscle power. Recently I saw the term *neurasthenia* used again. It was compared to M.E., the difference being that M.E. was associated with muscle pains.

The main cause of being tired all the time is trying to do too much, mentally or physically, but other causes of weakness include heart disease, cancer, blood disorders, glandular diseases especially a failure of the adrenal glands called Addison's disease, infectious diseases, kidney disease, liver disease and chronic pain such as in arthritis. Depression is another common cause. The point is that James means we should ask for prayer for any illness, it does not matter what.

'Weakness' in the Bible

Astheneo and its related words (*asthenes, astheneia* and *asthenema*) are used 67 times in the New Testament. In over one half of the references (including 12 times in the Epistles) the meaning is sickness or illness. Other meanings are: not strong, spiritually weak, weak conscience, shy, low self-esteem, helpless, unimpressive appearance, and weak flesh as opposed to the spirit. Some interesting examples are as follows:

1. Jesus sent his disciples to heal the sick (*astheneo*) as well as to preach, cleanse lepers, raise the dead and cast out devils (Matt. 10:7, 8).

2. In the parable of the sheep and the goats, Jesus said 'I was sick and you looked after me'. This meant illness as it was in a list including hunger, thirst, loneliness, nakedness and imprisonment. This passage incidentally is a powerful encouragement for those who look after the sick (Matt. 25:36).

3. Lazarus was *sick* (John 11). This was physical sickness because he died and was put in the tomb. Jesus raised him up.

4. Dorcas was *sick* and she died (Acts 9). Peter prayed for her and she was presented alive and well to the believers.

5. Paul had to leave Trophimus behind at Miletum *sick* (2 Tim. 4:20). Epaphroditus was *sick* almost unto death but God had mercy (Phil. 2:27). Timothy had frequent *sicknesses* (1 Tim. 5:23).

6. Christians can be weak (*astheneo*) in faith (Rom. 14:1) and in conscience (1 Cor. 8:7).

7. Many of the Christians in Corinth were *weak* and sickly and some were asleep because they had not recognised the Lord's body (1 Cor. 11:30). This could mean that they were weak spiritually and morally and so were ineffective as Christians (the word translated 'sickly' can mean moral weakness). Most commentators say that being asleep means they had died, so weak means being physically ill or invalids. Same or similar words are used for the girl being asleep in Mark 5:35-43 and in 1 Thessalonians 4:13-15. If this is so the Corinthians were asleep in Christ despite having sinned, which is very reassuring to me!

8. In 1 Corinthians 15, it is confirmed that our natural bodies are *weak* and so subject to disease, but verse 43 promises that our bodies will be raised in power when Jesus comes again.

9. Paul reminded the Galatians (Gal. 4:13) that the reason he was present to preach the gospel to them at the beginning was because of physical *weakness*. The inference was that the illness stopped him from doing something else. Perhaps because of the enforced stop, John Mark gave up in disgust and went home (Acts 13:13)!

10. Paul went to the Corinthians in *weakness* (*astheneia*), fear and much trembling (1 Cor. 2:3).

11. Said about Paul, 'his letters are severe and strong, but when he is with us in person, he is weak, and his words are nothing!' (2 Cor. 10:10, GNB).

12. Paul had to learn a lesson about *weakness*. This is found in the famous passage of his thorn in the flesh (2 Cor. 12:1-10). This suggests to me a stabbing pain, reminding me of the saying that shingles (herpes zoster) is a belt of roses from hell. Whatever it was it made him *weak*. It is very interesting that Paul was not healed of this weakness despite much prayer. The Lord told him that his power would be made perfect in *weakness*. We shall return to this but it is important to emphasise that it may not be God's will to heal in the way that we would like. Paul accomplished so much for his Lord. Would he have done so much in his own strength if he had been healed?

13. An amazing fact is that the Lord Jesus suffered weakness, again the same word *astheneo*. We read, 'He was crucified in weakness, yet he lives by God's power' (2 Cor. 13:4). Weakness here surely means both mental and physical. In the Garden of Gethsemane he was in anguish as he faced the horror to come, and no depressed patient has suffered as much as he did when his Father had to forsake him on the cross. As well as this our Saviour would have been very weak and ill, after the Roman flogging, as he struggled to get to Calvary. Truly a Man in pain and acquainted with weakness (Isaiah 53:3, using the words in Matthew 8). God did not heal his Son until the work of our redemption was done, until he could cry 'It is finished.'

There is another wonderful point here. Remember the story of Job. His afflictions included physical disease and he was tempted to curse God for causing his troubles (Job 2:9). Jesus must have been tempted by his sufferings, especially in the Garden of Gethsemane, to disobey his Father and give up the struggle. We read, however: 'He offered up prayers and petitions with loud cries and tears (there's weakness or sickness) ... he learned obedience from what he suffered' (Heb. 5:7,8). 'We do not have a high priest who is unable to sympathise with our weaknesses (*astheneo*) but we have one (Jesus) who has been tempted in every way (including illness or weakness), just as we are – yet without sin' (Heb. 4:15). Sympathise literally means 'to suffer with' – Jesus actually suffers with us in our weakness. We can reverently say that Jesus suffered illness but even in illness he resisted temptation. Some people say that Jesus did not suffer sickness, but surely he was not completely human if he did not at least get the common childhood illnesses. When we feel low due to illness and are tempted to say that God does not care, let us remind ourselves about Jesus and 'let us then approach the throne of grace with confidence, so that we may receive mercy and find grace to help us in our time of need' (Heb. 4:16).

The writer to the Hebrews presents the qualifications of a high priest (Heb. 5:1ff.). He was called of God from men. As a man he could have compassion because he himself was subject to weakness. Along with this weakness (*astheneo*), the high priest, being human, committed sins. He offered sacrifices for his own sins and the sins of the people. Jesus is a man, he is also the Son of God. He was called when he was a man to be the High Priest. Through his sufferings, including being tempted through human weakness, he learned obedience and was perfected as the Author of our salvation. God's plan is so wonderful, Jesus could not have been our perfect Saviour, unless he was sinless, which he was; and unless he experienced temptation through weakness like ours, which he did. In Hebrews 7:28 we read that the law appoints as high priests men who have weakness but by solemn oath God appoints the Son who has been perfected (through weakness) for ever.

The meaning of sickness (*astheneo*) in James

By using this word *astheneo*, James meant anything that causes weakness – nothing that we may suffer from is excluded. He meant physical disease, mental problems, shyness, low self-esteem, helplessness and spiritual problems. Paul wrote: 'When the body is buried, it is mortal; when raised, it will be immortal. When buried, it is ugly and weak; when raised, it will be beautiful and strong. When buried it is a physical body (natural, with weakness and disease); when raised, it will be a spiritual body (free of weakness and illness)' (1 Cor. 15:42-44, GNB, my words in parentheses). Illness is ugly, whether it is the wasting of cancer or the destruction of the mind in mental illness. The Living Bible has: 'The bodies we have now embarrass us, for they become sick and die; ... Yes, they are weak and dying bodies now.' 'Is any one of you sick' recognises the fact that our bodies and minds are frail and subject to disease. We are encouraged to ask the church for prayer.

Conclusion

The sick person is invited to ask the church for prayer. Physical, mental and spiritual problems are all included in James' invitation. The sick one does not need to fear rebuke as many Christians including Paul have been that way before him. Even his Saviour knows what it is like and he understands.

References

1. Hinton J., *Dying* Penguin. 1967.

2. Brown M.L., p.134, *Israel's Divine Healer,* Paternoster Press, 1995.

3. Horrox R., p.98, *The Black Death*, Manchester University Press, 1994.

4. Most of the material in this paragraph is from Horrox.

5. I am no Greek scholar. I am indebted to the following works for my understanding of Greek meanings:

   The Hebrew-Greek Study Bible ed. Zodhiates S. inc. Strong's dictionaries, Eyre and Spottiswoode/ AMG Publishers, 1984;

   The NKJV Greek English Interlinear New Testament, translators – Farstad A.L., Hodges Z.C., Moss C.M., Picirilli R.E., Pickering W.N., Thomas Nelson 1994;

   Vine's Complete Expository Dictionary of Old and New Testament Words, Vine W.E., Unger M.F. & White W.Jr., Thomas Nelson, 1985.

   Whenever there is a Greek word written in this book, the meanings are taken from these works. The only disagreement I found was over the meanings and occurrence of the various Greek words for 'sin'.

Chapter 3

THE CHURCH IN ACTION

He should call the elders of the church to pray over him and anoint him with oil in the name of the Lord.

The sick person has decided to ask for prayer. He has the faith to ask for prayer, though he does not know how the prayer will be answered. All he knows, and this is all that faith requires, is that he belongs to the Lord Jesus and that his heavenly Father loves him. In a sense he has put the onus on the church. He has given the church the responsibility to pray for him. Local churches should be ready to take this responsibility, and accept such requests.

The Elders

The sick one is to call the elders of the church. 'Elders' is a New Testament term for the leaders of the church. Elders were to keep watch, to look after the believers (Acts 20:28), and they were appointed or elected much the same as is done today. So by 'elders' we can include priests, rectors, ministers, pastors, elders and deacons, depending on our tradition. Why should he call the elders and not his closest friends in the church? We should understand that it is not because they are super-Christians or have greater faith. They do not. It is because they represent the whole body of believers. I think this is important, otherwise divisions may occur in the church. It may be that the sick one has had a difference of opinion with one of the elders in the past. Either or both may have been at fault, but relationships can also be healed during the ministry of healing. Obviously this would need great sensitivity by the elder concerned and would need to be included in the prayer preparation. The person responsible for responding to the call would need to consider if any such problems could arise.

It is important too that more than one elder answers the call. In my Baptist denomination, perhaps the minister and two or three deacons would go, the choice of deacons depending partly on their knowledge of the sick one. The number of elders is in accordance with our Lord's words in Matthew 18:19, where he says that if two agree, it will be done. In verse 20, he promises his presence where two or three come together in his Name. Agreement is vitally important when we consider the prayer of faith and indeed the Lord may give knowledge to one of the elders which can be considered by the others. This will be further discussed in the next chapter.

Through Christ
The call for prayer puts a great deal of responsibility onto the elders concerned. We all need to remind ourselves that it is through Christ that these things are done by the Holy Spirit. We have already seen how Paul was told that the Lord's power was made perfect in his weakness (2 Cor. 12:8), and Jesus himself told us that without him we can do nothing (John 15:5). The secret is to pray in the Spirit (Eph. 6:18), which means being filled with the Spirit, allowing him to have complete control over us. Obviously we should be in this state always but sin gets in the way and should be dealt with, which is why James later reminds us that we should confess our sins. Paul reminds us to keep on being filled with the Spirit, so he can influence our actions (Eph. 5:18). It is important, therefore, for the elders to prepare themselves before God in prayer and self-examination. All of us have an understandable anxiety and even horror as we confront serious illness in others and this will bring us to the Lord; especially if, as elders, we have been asked to visit.

In Unity
The other important thing about the elders is that they should be in unity (Eph. 4:3). It's not for nothing that the qualifications to be an elder include being gentle not quarrelsome (1 Tim. 3:3) and not

quick-tempered or overbearing (Titus 1:7). As the elders approach the sick one, how can they agree together in prayer if there is something wrong between them? There may therefore need to be some confessing of sins against each other in the group of elders. We all know that being responsible for the leadership of the church can produce disagreements; but unity is so very important.

Compassion

So the righteous, not self-righteous, group of elders arrive at the ill person's house. What do they do? First of all they need to be reasonably sure the sick one is a believer in the Lord Jesus Christ. If they are not sure they should still pray, but it is not fair to the sick to delude them. The promises in James are to believers. If this seems hard, remember that the sick person has himself asked the church for prayer so already must have some faith as we mentioned earlier. It may therefore be right for the elders to gently talk about the love of God and his acceptance of those who come to his Son for salvation. If, as is likely in these circumstances, the sick one is a Christian no harm is done. He will be greatly comforted by being reminded of the love of his Father:

> Tell me the story always,
> If you would really be,
> In any time of trouble,
> A comforter to me.

Preaching to the Sick

In case anyone has misunderstood me, I would like to digress a little at this point and talk about preaching the Christian message, the Good News, to the sick, especially the seriously ill.

Dr Martyn Lloyd-Jones said the reason why he ended his medical career was because he felt he was getting people well to sin again.[1] He said that when he told the sick about their immortal souls they promised grand things but when they got better they sinned again. I admire him for that. I do believe in preaching the gospel of Jesus Christ and challenging people, but I do not think it is my role at the sick-bed. I do not usually warn the dying about eternal issues. My role as a doctor is to alleviate suffering and pain to the best of my ability. This will often mean the use of morphine and heroin in high doses. Experienced staff in hospices have shown that pain can often be relieved without clouding the consciousness but sedation is often needed to relieve distress.[2] It is very difficult for someone in such a situation to consider the Christian message. We should always remember that in ourselves we cannot save anybody. We believe in an all-loving, all-knowing God who has chosen who is to be 'holy in his sight' from before the foundation of the world (Eph. 1:4). It is possible for someone to be saved on their deathbed, I think if that is to happen God will make it very clear. Bishop Ryle, in his comments about the two men who were crucified with Jesus, said that one man was saved almost at the point of death, so that no-one should despair.[3] He also said, only one, so that none should presume. The message is that we should accept Jesus as Saviour today, while we are well, because tomorrow, when we are ill, we may not be able to. If another's salvation depended on us then we would be right to worry but, praise God, it doesn't. Will not the Judge of all the earth do right (Gen. 18:25)? We should bring all these things before God in secret. I remember worrying very much about a young woman who was dying from cancer. While I was driving to see her, I was praying and I believe the Lord reassured me that I was not to worry. Her relationship to God was unknown to me but he told me to leave it with him. Our Lord is full of compassion, and he has used illness to bring someone to him. I accept that other Christian doctors, like Dr Lloyd-Jones, may have different views to me about preaching to the sick. I respect their position and I do not want to be dogmatic about it, but want to act as the Lord leads me.

It is often very useful to involve the local minister or priest. In this country many people have at least a nominal allegiance to a certain denomination, and they will welcome a visit by 'their' minister. Such a person, whatever their doctrinal position, is usually excellent in talking of the love of God. One hospital chaplain said that ministering to patients led him to offer the simple but profound message of God's unconditional love and led him to believe that the realisation of this in a person's life is a conversion experience.[4]

In Love

James says the elders are to pray over the sick person, the idea being that they surround him or her in love, a beautiful picture of the all-enveloping love of God. They are to pray in the name of the Lord. I understand that in this sentence, 'in the name of the Lord' applies more to the prayer than the anointing. In other words, pray in the name of the Lord, having anointed with oil.[5] 'In his name' means praising him – our Lord Jesus – seeking his will, accepting his will, obeying his will in unity. Remember it may not be his will to remove the illness. The prayer is accompanied by anointing with oil, usually a smear of olive oil on the forehead.

Anointing with Oil

Oil was used as a dressing, it is a natural emollient or softener, and so some people take the anointing to mean the use of medicines. Rabbinic sources, following Old Testament usage, prescribe the use of oil for the treatment of sciatica, skin afflictions, headaches and wounds.[6] Liquid paraffin or petroleum jelly is commonly used in dressings for superficial wounds today. The Good News Bible translates 'anoint' to mean rub with oil because the Greek word for anoint means a physical act. The touching of the person can of course be very comforting. The word has a deeper spiritual meaning and is used in the Greek translation of the Old Testament to describe the ceremonial consecration of the priests to God's service (Exod. 40:15). Moo suggests that James' meaning is therefore a physical action with symbolic significance.[7]

Anointing, then, speaks about setting apart the sick one for God, for him to use. How can an ill person be useful to God? By showing that he trusts in God, by accepting his will, he shows or proclaims to others the glory and loving care of God. If in adversity we praise God, this is a powerful witness to the reality of our faith. In his suffering, Job did not understand the purposes of God but his desperate cry, in the mistaken belief that God might kill him, confirms his faith and his God. 'Though he slay me, yet will I hope in him' (Job 13:15).

When is the right time to pray?

The simplest answer is when the sick person asks. But there are certain times during an illness when the right time to pray has certainly come. Some of these are: when the illness is diagnosed; just before an operation; before any uncomfortable treatment such as chemotherapy; and when and if the disease relapses after initial treatment. We should ask God that side effects of treatment will be minimal.

We should also, I think, ask for prayer for chronic illness and disability such as arthritis. Surgical treatment of osteo-arthritis, especially of the hips, is one of the triumphs of modern medicine for which we can thank God. James would have had no inkling of this, of course, but I think he would have approved of the elders meeting before such routine 'cold' surgery to ask that everything would go smoothly without complications.

Finally, I do not see there is any justification in James for leaving prayer and anointing until a 'last rites'. The promise in James is expectancy of healing according to the will of God.

Conclusion

What is the purpose in calling the elders? It is so they can call on God for the sick person because he is too weak to do so himself. It is to help him to commit himself completely to God, to help him to know God's love and care afresh. This means that even if the illness is not healed, he knows his heavenly Father has heard and answered by the very fact that he is at peace in his love.

References

1. Murray I.H., *Dr. D Martyn Lloyd-Jones: The First Forty Years* p.80, Banner of Truth Trust, 1982.

2. Smith A.M., p.47, *Gateway to Life*, Inter-Varsity Press, 1994.

3. Ryle J.C., p.244, *Practical Religion*, James Clarke, 1959.

4. Woodroffe I., *Towards a Hospice Theology* quoted in *Mud and Stars*, p.167, Twycross R. et. al., Sobell Publications, 1991.

5. Zodhiates S., p.1513, *Hebrew-Greek Key Study Bible*, Eyre and Spottiswoode/AMG, 1984.

6. John J. in *The Oil of Gladness* p.50, Dudley M. & Rowell G. Eds., SPCK, 1993, includes references.

7. Moo D.J., p.180, *James*, Tyndale New Testament Commentaries, Inter-Varsity Press, 1985.

Chapter 4

THE PRAYER IN FAITH

And the prayer offered in faith will make the sick person well;
the Lord will raise him up.

I said earlier that this chapter is the most important in the book. This is because it will deal with the prayer *of* or *in* faith.

In the last chapter we discussed praying in the name of the Lord. Now we have the prayer in faith; and I would like to add prayer in the Spirit (Eph. 6:18; Jude 20). Ultimately all three phrases mean the same thing, you cannot have one without the others. Believing prayer is in the name of the Lord Jesus Christ through the Holy Spirit to the heavenly Father.

Faith – Belief in (or on) the Lord Jesus

If someone comes to us and asks the way of salvation, what do we say? Paul's answer to the jailer was: 'Believe in the Lord Jesus, and you will be saved' (Acts 16:31). We all know that this does not just mean we know about Jesus Christ. It means more than believing he was born in Bethlehem, more even than believing he rose from the dead or that he is coming again, even though it includes all that. When I call him, 'Lord Jesus Christ', I mean he, who was sent by God to save me, is now my Lord. Believing in the Lord Jesus means that we utterly depend on him for salvation and give him our total allegiance as Lord. That is why we use terms like 'giving your heart to the Lord Jesus', the very centre of your being. 'For it is with your heart that you believe and are justified' (Rom. 10:10).

I am sure that every Christian believer has doubts from time to time about their salvation. The devil is always seeking to undermine our faith. In my own experience these attacks of doubt have got less the longer I have been a Christian because I have experience of God at work. I am even more certain that each believer has times when God is very near and then there is no doubt at all. There is a God-given certainty of being saved, of being a child of God. This is faith.

People sometimes accuse evangelical Christians of being too dogmatic. Surely, they say, it is presumptuous to claim a personal relationship with Almighty God. I would agree, were it not for the fact that Almighty God has himself formed the relationship. How then are we certain of our salvation? Firstly, because God is true to his Word as given to us in the Bible. Such verses as John 3:16, Acts 16:31 and Romans 10:9 are astounding in their simplicity but also in their truth. Secondly, we can be certain of our salvation because God reveals these truths to us personally. The Bible itself admits that the message of the cross is nonsense to the unsaved but to those who are saved it shows the power of God (1 Cor. 1:18). This change in outlook must come from God to us. This is the work of the Holy Spirit. We do not need to be paralysed by fear of the future because we can call God, Father. His Holy Spirit confirms to us that we are his children and so joint heirs with Christ (Rom. 8:15-17). We know for certain that we will share in God's glory (2 Tim. 1:12). This would be breath-taking audacity were it not for the fact that none of this knowledge, none of this certainty, depends on us. It is all given to us by God. Paul's words in Timothy are used in Daniel Whittle's great hymn:

> I know not why God's wondrous grace
> To me has been made known;
> Nor why – unworthy as I am –
> He claimed me for his own.

> But 'I know whom I have believed; and
> am persuaded that he is able to keep that
> which I've committed unto him against that day.'

> I know not how this saving faith
> To me he did impart;
> Or how believing in his word
> Wrought peace within my heart.

This has been the experience of countless Christians down the centuries. Saving faith then is the certainty or even guarantee of eternal life with God.

Faith – Belief in Prayer

All the above is familiar. The same principles apply to faith in prayer as they do to faith in salvation. Just as we cannot create or work up faith in our salvation, even so we cannot create or work up faith in our prayers. Prayer in faith is the God-given certainty that what we ask for will happen.

How does the Bible define faith? 'Faith is being sure of what we hope for and certain of what we do not see' (Heb. 11:1). 'Being sure' is the NIV translation of a word meaning: the foundation of; the guarantee of; the deed of covenant of; the substance of. In other words something is going to happen in the future and faith sees it as if it has already happened. It is as if faith has been to the future on a time machine and has seen what will happen. Because we have faith given by God that something we hope for will happen, our faith is the guarantee.

Faith is also being certain of what we do not see. Being certain means having evidence of, having proof, being convicted of the truth of something. The Greek word for 'being certain' is also used in 2 Timothy 3:16. This says 'All Scripture is God-breathed and is useful for teaching, *rebuking,* etc.' 'Rebuking' or 'reproof' seems a completely different word to 'being certain', but the basic idea is conviction in a court of law. When a criminal is so convicted, the charges against him are proven, his guilt is certain and the law rebukes him. So being certain of what we do not see, is to be convinced of an unseen, but hoped for, truth and accepting that that truth applies to us.

Putting these two things together, we can say faith that something will happen is the guarantee and proof that it will happen and the conviction that it applies to us. We can immediately see there is, therefore, no way that faith can be worked up. There is only One who knows such detail, and so faith must be a gift from God. The Bible confirms this: 'you have been saved through faith – and this not from yourselves, it is the gift of God' (Eph. 2:8). Peter talks about receiving faith and adding to that faith (2 Pet.1:1, 5); and Paul advises us to be honest with ourselves in accordance with the amount of faith God has given us (Rom. 12:3). In his statement of the mustard seed Jesus said that even a small amount of faith can do great things (Matt. 17:20). It is no wonder if God gives that faith. The father of the boy with the evil spirit said 'I do believe; help me overcome my unbelief!', in other words he asked for more faith (Mark 9:24).

Prayer in Faith is in the Name of the Lord

I stated above that prayer in faith is the same as prayer in the name of the Lord and the same as prayer in the Spirit. Now we have considered what faith is, we can see that this is true. Prayer in the name of the Lord will be according to the will of God, so the faith will be given. The words of our Lord Jesus are very clear: 'In my name ... they (those who believe) will place their hands on sick people and they will get well' (Mark 16:17, 18); 'Have faith in God (or be persuaded by God) ... Therefore I tell you, whatever you ask for in prayer, believe that you have received it, and it will be yours' (Mark 11:22-24). Jesus went on to remind us to forgive other people when we come to God in prayer. He also said: 'You may ask me for anything in my name, and I will do it. If you love me, you will obey what I command' (John 14:14, 15). There is another point here, if a request is in his name we need to obey and pray. If it is in God's will to heal a person, it is disobedient not to pray for that healing. When we consider these things it is reassuring and humbling to know that God has already prepared what good works we should do (Eph. 2:10). If it is his will to heal, he will prepare somebody to pray for that healing. That person must be ready to obey.

Why does God answer our prayers? Obviously, it is to bring glory to his name, but Jesus also said it is to give us great joy. 'Until now you have not asked for anything in my name. Ask and you will receive, and your joy will be complete' (John 16:24). How good God is to us. As we pray in his name we will be very happy as we see our prayers answered. As this happens our faith will grow; in other words, God will entrust to us more of his will. C. H. Spurgeon, the famous preacher of the nineteenth century, used the term 'chequebook of the bank of faith'. I have a bank credit card that I do not use very much but recently have used it more. The Bank has immediately increased my credit limit! As we step out and use our faith, God will increase our credit in the bank of faith – he will increase our faith and use us more. Unlike my bank we do not have to pay back! George Müller, caring for orphans in Bristol in the last century, abundantly confirmed this, as with no income, he was able to feed the children, receiving the funds daily by faith.

Prayer in Faith is in the Spirit

Prayer in faith in the name of the Lord is also in the Holy Spirit. Jude said 'build yourselves up in your most holy faith and pray in the Holy Spirit' (Jude 20). After the passage on the armour of God, Paul told us to 'pray in the Spirit on all occasions with all kinds of prayers and requests' (Eph. 6:18). How do we pray in the Spirit? Again by being obedient, doing God's will, waiting on him by prayer and reading his Word to discover what we should pray for.

Sometimes we do not know what we should pray for, sometimes the Lord does not reveal it to us. I know this will happen as we tend the sick. Then we should pray as well as we can; and the Bible promises us that the Spirit himself will pray for us with groans that words cannot express (Rom. 8:26). I think the point here is, as we stand at the sick-bed, we groan within us with pity and love as we see the suffering of the sick one and the Holy Spirit takes that up. It all depends on how genuine is our concern, for verse 27 goes on: 'And he (the Father) who searches our hearts knows the mind of the Spirit (or – he knows the spiritual mind?), because the Spirit intercedes for the saints in accordance with God's will.' The Father sees how genuine we are and so our poor stumbling prayers are transformed by the Spirit into the correct prayer for that need. This again should fill us with wonder and praise. If we are finding it difficult to pray for somebody, even as we are struggling to do so, we can rest assured that the Holy Spirit is doing a perfect job on our behalf! I should mention here, for some Christians, such prayer may include speaking in tongues. That is what Paul meant when he said 'I will pray with my spirit, but I will also pray with my mind' (1 Cor. 14:15). You do not need to speak in tongues to pray in the Spirit, but if someone has the gift of tongues this will be helpful. I think caution is needed when praying in tongues with the sick, for if the sick one does not understand, how can he share in the prayer? The important thing is to be in unity and in love. As we think about the sick-bed I think it is helpful to consider parts of 1 Corinthians 13:

'If I speak in the tongues of men and of angels, but have not love, I am only a resounding gong or a clanging cymbal. If I have ... all knowledge and if I have a faith that can move mountains, but have not love, I am nothing ....
     Love is patient, love is kind ... it is not proud .... It always protects, always trusts, always hopes, always perseveres ....
     Love never fails ....
     Now I know in part; then I shall know fully ....
     And now these three remain: FAITH, HOPE and LOVE. But the greatest of these is love.'

The results of the Prayer in Faith

'And the prayer offered in faith will make the sick person well'. To re-iterate, we cannot manufacture or work up faith. I think we can also say that initially the healing faith is given to the elders rather than to the sick one. This is apparent from the accounts of healing in Acts: for example, in Acts 3 the lame man was very surprised to be healed. However, he had to make the effort to jump to his feet. This suggests that to be blessed by the healing ministry, a person must commit himself to God. There have been examples of people healed who are not believers. If this is true, if that person does not then commit himself to God, ultimately the healing is worthless.

A person can quench the work of the Holy Spirit; but if the sick person is accepting God's will, this will not happen. I want to emphasise as strongly as I can that if the sick person is not healed it is not his fault. It is very cruel to tell the sick that they were not healed because of their lack of faith, as if they could make faith. No, they were not healed because the faith to be healed was not given, and the faith was not given because it was not God's will.

By his knowledge and wisdom, God wills that something will happen and therefore it will happen. God is not limited by time, so he sees things in the future as if they have already happened. The wisdom of God leads to an action of God, say healing. Because God sees healing in the future as already accomplished, he gives to his servant the faith to pray for that healing. The mystery is that he appears to need our prayer, or rather, he has deigned to include our prayer. The analogy of Chemistry comes to my mind. GCSE students understand the necessity of balancing a chemical equation. Let's call this the equation of healing :

GOD'S WISDOM AND GOD'S WILL———→ HEALING AND FAITH
but that is not balanced, the balanced equation is:

GOD'S WISDOM + WILL + OUR PRAYERS ——→ HEALING + FAITH
that is still not right because our faith leads to prayer so we have a cycle :

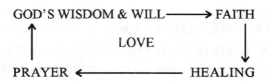

Faith leads to healing but also healing leads to faith. The important point I am trying to get to in this cycle is that all these things are related to and depend on each other. The hub of the cycle, the centre of things is love.

The Guidance of the Holy Spirit

As we pray for the sick person we need to pray carefully allowing the Holy Spirit to lead us. It is wrong and condemned by God to claim healing when no assurance of this is given, which is why three people have to agree on what to pray for. As the elders gather to pray for the sick person I think there are two possibilities:

1. They are not given the knowledge and certainty by the Spirit that complete healing will occur – they are not given the faith. They will still pray in faith but according to the faith that they have been given. This will mean commending the sick one to God, asking for his grace, help and comfort, asking for healing according to his will. I see nothing wrong in saying to God, 'If it is your will'. This is not a cop-out, just uncertainty. I am sure the Lord will bless such an honest prayer.

   OR

2. They are given the certainty by the Holy Spirit that the person will be healed and so they will boldly pray the prayer in faith for healing. They will expect healing to occur and so I believe will the sick one.

Roger Barrier wrote: 'The prayer of faith can only be prayed when God speaks to reveal his will and intention. When I pray for people who come to the elders, I usually have no idea what God intends to do in their situation. Occasionally, God makes his will known clearly. In those latter cases it is exciting to pray a prayer of faith – and watch God work.'[1]

Wrestling in prayer

There is a time for so called wrestling with God, pleading with him for the answer we want. The best examples are Abraham and Jacob. Abraham pleaded for the righteous in Sodom and Gomorrah and he gradually reduced the threshold of the number of righteous for the cities to be saved from fifty to ten (Gen. 18:16-33). Jacob actually wrestled with God until he gave him a blessing (Gen. 32:22-32). In each case it is obvious afterwards that they did not change God's mind; rather, God was testing them. There is no doubt that Paul pleaded with God for the nation of Israel (Rom. 9:1-3). The Lord Jesus himself advised us to persist in prayer almost as if we make nuisances of ourselves (Luke 11:5-13). He said, 'keep on asking, keep on seeking, keep on knocking.' We need to have an urgency and persistence in prayer; but as far as praying for the sick is concerned this pleading should be done in private, not at the sick-bed. Jesus also said, 'When you pray, go into your room, close the door and pray to your Father' (Matt. 6:6).

God is sovereign

The true approach to the prayer in faith, is to accept that God is sovereign and that he knows best. We are to come to him, with our hearts and minds open and ready to receive, without any preconditions or demands. He will then give us the faith to pray for what is in his Will and Wisdom. We can rest assured that we will not be turned away empty handed – he loves us so much.

What if God does not give the faith to pray for physical healing?

As I said in chapter 1, this is the experience of many people. Others have accused them of unbelief, sin or not being patient, not waiting on the Lord. We should remember that God never says *no*, but he does say *not yet*. The answer may only come in heaven. The believer knows that one day, all his hurts, all his pain, all his weakness, all his illness will be healed. That is a certainty to the one who is born again, who is adopted into the family of God. I believe that God will always give healing in answer to prayer, but the healing may be peace and contentment in his will.

God is sovereign but he is also full of compassion. There is no doubt at all that sometimes he heals miraculously when we least expect it. In other words, when we have not prayed the prayer of faith. Many people with experience of healing confirm this. All we can say is that the Lord's compassion does not negate his wisdom. If we pray for healing with little faith, and healing wonderfully occurs, then the healing is still 'right'. There is no way that we can persuade God to do what is wrong. God sometimes heals despite our lack of faith; or rather, he sometimes heals despite us not accepting the faith that he wants to give. This is wonderful for the sick one, of course, but it does not build up the church because the healing can so easily be put down to natural remission or a host of other medical explanations. The Lord may deign to heal unexpectedly, according to his inscrutable wisdom; but I believe the normal way he has ordained for the church is through James 5.

There is one seemingly incontrovertible point that people make. They say that if you do not believe that it is God's will to heal or cure your illness, then you should not seek medical help or even take painkillers. I think this is so sadly mistaken. Such people do not understand the nature of sickness. Some conditions that cause hurt, sadness and illness are inherited. A good example is Down's Syndrome. I do not believe it would be God's will to cure such a person by giving them normal chromosomes. That is what curing would mean. But it would be ridiculous to say that because a Down's sufferer is not cured, therefore they should not receive medical care. This can be repeated for many many illnesses. Because it is not God's will to restore somebody's amputated leg, does that mean that an ulcer on the stump caused by the artificial limb should not be treated? So much medical work means caring, alleviating, helping without strictly curing.

I have been greatly blessed as I have considered what praying in faith means. Let us go forward, getting rid of the sins that get in the way, walking in the Spirit that we may discern the will of God. I pray that this may be so.

References

1. Barrier R., *A Pastor's View of Praying for the Sick*, esp. p.225 in *The Kingdom and the Power*, ed. Greig G.S. & Springer K.N., Regal Books, 1993.

I wish to note here that the following books were of great help in my understanding of the prayer in faith:

MacNutt F., *Healing*, Fowler Wright Books Ltd., 1974.

Moo D.J. *James* Tyndale Commentaries. IVP/Eerdmans 1985

Motyer A., *The Message of James*, IVP, 1985.

Since I wrote this chapter, I have obtained *Sent to Heal* by Harold Taylor, Order of St Luke the Physician, Australasia, 1993. Taylor quotes from C.S. Storms, *Healing and Holiness*, Presbyterian and Reformed, 1990, who has similar thoughts about the prayer in faith.

I also acknowledge and recommend *The Kingdom and the Power*, especially the chapter by Barrier (see above).

Chapter 5

SAVED AND HEALED

'And the prayer offered in faith will make the sick person well;
the Lord will raise him up' (NIV).
'And the prayer of faith shall save the sick,
and the Lord shall raise him up' (AV).
'This prayer made in faith will heal the sick person;
the Lord will restore him to health' (GNB)

I have quoted the three versions above to try and bring out the meaning of James' verse; 'will make the sick person well' (NIV); 'shall save the sick' (AV); and 'will heal the sick person' (GNB). They are translations of the same Greek word *sozo*. This word is used many times in the New Testament. Indeed, whenever we see the words 'save', 'saviour', 'salvation' in our English versions, they are all from this word. The most important use of this word is in relation to salvation from our sins, the healing of our broken relationship with God, our spiritually dead natures made whole. We hear a lot today about holistic medicine, the treatment of the whole man: mind, body and spirit. The Bible is well ahead of this, *sozo* does apply to body, soul and spirit. I think James used this word carefully here, I think he intended it to have a whole man or woman meaning. He did not mean exclusively spiritual salvation for we have already confirmed that he is talking to Christians. Most commentators agree that James is talking about saving or healing from illness, but he does not neglect the spiritual aspect. I understand a word for word translation is: 'The prayer of faith will save the one being ill.'

Jesus the Healer[1]

I think we can illustrate James' use of *sozo* by looking at the scriptures. Excluding the raising of the dead and the healing of crowds, there are twenty-four recorded instances of Jesus healing individuals. Sometimes special words are used such as cleansing (of lepers), restoration, setting free and making straight. That leaves eleven instances where we read that Jesus healed or made whole. In only four of them is the word *sozo* used as far as I can tell. Incidentally where healings are mentioned in more than one Gospel account the same word is often used. Another word for 'healing' is *iaomai*. The Greek word for doctor is *iatros*, from which we get our words paediatrics (healing or medical care of children) and psychiatry (healing of the mind). Other words are *therapeuo*, therapeutics in English; *hygies* and *holokleria* for made whole, from which we get hygiene and holistic. The use of the word *sozo* is special. When the disciples were sent to heal, *sozo* is never used (e.g. Matt. 10:1); and it is not usually used when Jesus healed crowds. A possible exception is Matthew 14:36 (also Mark 6:56), but even here it is a derivative of *sozo* meaning saving from (the disease) or delivered from or made whole.

The four cases of the use of *sozo* are the demon possessed man called Legion (Luke 8:26-39); the woman with bleeding (Matt. 9:20-22; Mark 5:25-34; Luke 8:43-48 – *sozo* is used in all three versions); blind Bartimaeus (Mark 10:46-52; Luke 18:35-43 – both use *sozo*); and the ten men with leprosy (Luke 17:1-19). To these can be added two other cases from the Acts of the Apostles: the lame man at the gate (Acts 3) and the crippled man in Lystra (Acts 14:8-10). In both instances *sozo* is used. Let me present their case histories. To make it more understandable I have invented some possible personal details but have not altered the important facts.

1. Mr. L. (Legion) (Luke 8:26-39)

History: Severe psychotic mental illness for a long time.

Past History: Attempts had been made to chain him up under guard but he had broken away. Lived naked in the graveyard.

Diagnosis: Demon possession.

Treatment: The demons were driven out. He was clothed and his mental illness was healed.

Discussion: Poor Legion had a severe mental disorder caused by Satan. We do not know how this happened. Attempts had been made to chain him up. This was a very common fate for mentally ill people in the past. Legion's illness possibly would be diagnosed as severe paranoid schizophrenia today. He would be very difficult to treat. Most cases of schizophrenia are not caused by demon possession but the Bible says he was possessed. Jesus cast the demons out and he was cured (*sozo*, Luke 8:36). Jesus told him to go home and tell everybody what God had done for him.

2. Mrs. A. aged 36 (Mark 5:25-34)

History: Metrorrhagia (heavy irregular vaginal bleeding) for twelve years.

Past History: Investigation and treatment by many doctors with no improvement.

Family and Social History: Poverty and estrangement from family.

Diagnosis: Uterine disease complicated by fear, depression and loneliness.

Treatment: Healing, salvation, peace, freedom and restoration to family.

Discussion: This poor woman was an outcast because of her condition but she thought that if she touched Jesus' clothes she would be healed (*sozo*). We are told that immediately her bleeding stopped and she was healed (*iaomai*). Jesus graciously spoke to her and said, 'Daughter, your faith has healed you (*sozo*). Go in peace and be freed from your suffering.' From the words used, he gave her physical healing, *iaomai*; complete healing or salvation, *sozo*; peace, *eirene*; and freedom or complete health, wholeness, *hygies*. According to the law such a woman was avoided, but Jesus accepted her, calling her 'Daughter'. Not only was she healed, after seven days she would be able to rejoin her family (Lev. 15:25-30).

3. **Mr. B. (Bartimaeus)** (Mark 10:46-52)

History: Blindness.

> *Social History*: Unable to work, poverty, surviving by begging.

> *Treatment*: Sight restored and a new direction in life.

> *Discussion*: Jesus said to him, 'Your faith has healed you' (*sozo*).

We are told that immediately he received his sight and followed Jesus along the road. As Bartimaeus had recognised Jesus as the Son of David (Mark 10:47), so he now recognised him as his Saviour. He followed him along the road, that is, along the Christian way. Luke says he followed Jesus, praising God (Luke 18:43).

4. **Mr. C.** (Luke 17:11-19)

History: Leprosy, possibly Hansen's disease, for many years.

> *Social History*: Outcast because of the law. Living rough with nine other sufferers in the countryside. Samaritan.

> *On Examination*: Swellings on face especially around eyes. Pale numb patches on skin. Deformity of feet and hands with some loss of fingers and toes.

> *Treatment*: Complete healing of disease, restoration to society and salvation.

> *Discussion*: Ten men with leprosy asked Jesus to help them. To the ancients, a label of leprosy brought as much fear and loathing

as AIDS does to many today. Leprosy in the Bible and in the Middle Ages was a hotch-potch of conditions. True Leprosy or Hansen's disease may have been one of the conditions, especially in the Middle Ages and possibly at the time of Jesus. The original Hebrew word translated as leprosy means 'smitten of God'. One medieval quote runs: 'For just as leprosy makes the body ugly, loathsome and monstrous, so the filth of lechery makes the soul very loathsome spiritually, and the swelling of secret pride is leprosy, that no man may hide.' Lepers were supposed to have uncontrollable sexual urges. On the other hand, sex during menstrual bleeding was supposed to result in leprous offspring, which is an interesting comment on the plight of the woman in case 2, at least to the medieval mind.[2]

It is very sad that even in recent times these old beliefs have caused prejudice against people with leprosy. Leprosy or Hansen's disease is an infectious illness just like, say, tuberculosis, being caused by a bacterium called Mycobacterium Leprae. It is not a sexually transmitted disease at all.

Although society loathed those with leprosy in Bible times, Jesus accepted them but he tested their faith by telling them to show themselves to the priests. Only the priests could pronounce someone was cured from leprosy. As they went they were cleansed. This word, 'cleansed' – *kathariso* from which we get our word 'catharsis' – is used in the Bible only in healing from leprosy except where it is used in cleansing from sin (e.g.1 John 1:9). Only one of the ten turned back and worshipped Jesus. Jesus said to him, 'Rise and go; your faith has made you well', or saved you (*sozo*).

5. **Mr. X. Age about 40** (Acts 3–4)

History: Crippled from birth.

Social History: Beggar but he had friends who carried him every day to the temple gate.

Treatment: Healing, soundness, wholeness and salvation.

Discussion: The healing of this man caused a lot of excitement in Jerusalem because he was well known. Nearly two chapters in Acts are occupied by his story and the aftermath. A number of words are used to describe his healing: complete healing in 3:16; healing (*sozo*) in 4:9, and different words again in verses 10 and 14. After he was healed he went into the temple courts, walking and jumping and praising God.

6. **Mr. Y. from Lystra** (Acts 14:8-10)

History: Crippled from birth, possibly talipes equino-varus (severe club foot).

Treatment: Healing and salvation.

Discussion: At Lystra we are told that Paul was preaching the good news, telling the people about Jesus, his death and resurrection and how he wanted to save them if only they would accept him as Lord. Mr. Y. was listening carefully to this and Paul saw by means of the Holy Spirit that he had faith to be healed or saved (*sozo*). Paul told him to stand up and he walked. I think we are justified in thinking that he became a Christian.

The accounts of these six healings describe more than physical or mental healing. In each case there was a deeper spiritual healing. The most striking case was the ten men with leprosy. All of them received cleansing from the disease, but only one received the deeper healing or salvation meant by the word *sozo*. I think then that when we see the use of this word, as in James 5:15, it means more than physical or mental healing although it includes that. It means healing or saving of mind, body and/or spirit depending on the context.

By his Wounds we are Healed

There is another very important connection between saving and healing that we see in the atonement of our Lord Jesus Christ for our sins. The theme of healing starts in Exodus when God said to the Israelites: 'I am the LORD, who heals you' (Exod. 15:26). Although there were special circumstances in the desert, this verse is a demonstration of an eternal truth that healing is an attribute of God. We then see a connection between forgiveness and healing in Psalm 103:3: 'who (the Lord) forgives all your sins and heals all your diseases'. The clearest expression though is in Isaiah 53:4-5, the sufferings of the Servant, the Messiah, our Lord Jesus Christ:

> Surely he took up our infirmities
> and carried our sorrows,
> yet we considered him stricken by God
> smitten by him and afflicted.
> But he was pierced for our transgressions,
> he was crushed for our iniquities;
> the punishment that brought us peace was upon him
> and by his wounds we are healed.

'Infirmities' has also been translated as pains or griefs or indeed sickness; and 'sorrows' is from a Hebrew word meaning physical and mental pain or disease. This passage, together with Psalm 22, has always meant a great deal to Christians as we think of what our Lord suffered as he obtained our salvation. We can also see that it includes a promise of healing from sickness. This is borne out by Matthew's account of driving out evil spirits and healing the sick, when he said that Isaiah's words were fulfilled: 'He took up our infirmities and carried our diseases' (Matt. 8:17).

We can say, therefore, that our Lord Jesus carried the burden of our sins and of our sicknesses on the cross. Death we are told is the wages of sin (Rom. 6:23); and this is physical and spiritual. Sin leads to spiritual death; while sickness leads to physical death. 'For as in Adam all die [physically and spiritually], so in Christ all will be made alive' [physically and spiritually] (1 Cor. 15:22). There is, therefore, a connection between sickness and sin and Christ died for both. The difference is that sickness is something that happens to us; while sin, although happening to us, is also and very importantly something we do.

The victory won by our Lord Jesus is against death. 'Death has been swallowed up in victory' (1 Cor. 15:54). However although the ultimate victory is assured, the battle continues. As we can never be completely free from sin until we have a new body in heaven; so we cannot be immune from every disease. Thomas À Kempis wrote: 'So long as we inhabit this frail body we can never be without sin or live without weakness and pain. We would gladly have rest and freedom from all misery, but, having lost our innocence by sin, we have also lost our true blessedness ... till mortality be swallowed up in life!'[3] Paul said: 'Meanwhile we groan, longing to be clothed with our heavenly dwelling' [i.e. body] (2 Cor. 5:2). The promise is secure: in heaven there will be no sin; but neither will there be tears, death, mourning, crying or pain (Rev. 21:4). The Lord, in his mercy, encourages us by sometimes healing but always comforting, so giving us a foretaste of glory when he will wipe every tear from our eyes.

'Come to me all you who are weary'

'Is any one of you sick' from James 5:14. (Prayer in faith) 'will make the sick person well' from verse 15.

Let us return to our phrase: the prayer in faith will make the sick person well, will heal or save the sick person. There is a change of word, here, which I think is significant. James is again choosing his words carefully. The word for sick in verse 14 was *astheneo*, weakness; while the word translated in every version as sick in verse 15, is *kamno*, to be weary. Weariness is often an accompaniment of severe illness leading on to depression and hindering recovery. There is the expression about the ill, 'turning their faces to the wall', giving up. All doctors have seen this many times. To the Christian this is not the same as merciful release into the arms of God, but is a very sad situation. Praying for the sick will avoid this happening. I have a hope that all Christian people can be at peace when they pass away, which I think is one of the reasons for this passage and indeed, one reason why I wanted to write this book.

Kamno is also used in the Greek translation of Job 10:1: 'I am sickened of life; I shall give free rein to my complaints, speaking out in the bitterness of my soul' (REB). The writer of Hebrews gives us this advice, 'Consider [Jesus] who endured such opposition from sinful men, so that you will not grow weary (*kamno*) and lose heart' (Heb. 12:3). This is the very idea that James is suggesting. How lovely it is to look at Jesus whatever trouble we are in. It is my conviction that prayer for the sick, in this manner, will help them to look away from their illness unto Jesus, the author and perfecter of our faith. The prayer in faith will make the sick person well; will comfort the weary; will heal the bitter in heart.

Wake up to the Love of God

The next phrase to consider is 'the Lord will raise him up'. The word used here is *egeiro* which means to 'wake up', as well as to 'raise up'. From what I have written so far, we could translate James 5:15 as, 'the prayer in faith will heal the weary, depressed, sick person; the Lord will raise him up'. *Egeiro* has a number of uses in the New Testament: to wake up from normal sleep (Matt. 1:24); to wake up to or realise a danger (Rom. 13:11); to raise or help a sick person up (Mark 1:31; 9:27); to raise from the dead (1 Cor. 6:14); and also to appear (Matt. 24:11). Obviously, then, the meaning could be that the Lord will raise, lift up or help up the sick one from the bed, meaning that he gets better, emphasising that it is the Lord who is healing.

I like the idea of 'waking up'. Let us go back to the sick person being weary or depressed. One of the clinical features of severe depression is extreme tiredness or lethargy, with a feeling of hopelessness, so much so that the person can appear doped. This is probably why the natural response to a depressed person is to say 'wake your ideas up' or 'pull yourself together'. Such a person is withdrawn into himself. What I think James is saying here is that the Lord wakes or raises up such a sufferer. The picture is of someone with his head hanging down, perhaps even with self pity, and the Lord gently lifts his chin up to look at him. Extreme weariness is also, so often, the condition of someone with terminal cancer. I should add that extreme weariness, in someone with cancer, can be due to severe pain. I have seen remarkable transformations in people when their pain is relieved. I like something that Andrew Murray wrote in the late nineteenth century. I don't agree with him that all illness can be attributed to personal sin, and I don't agree that all Christians can be free of all illness, but he was not wrong in writing this about self pity. The reason I say this is because this passage greatly encouraged me in my illness:

> How many more are there who are drawn by the sickness itself to be constantly occupied with themselves and with the condition of their body? What infinite care they exercise in observing the least symptom, favourable or unfavourable .... How much they are taken up with what they consider is due to them from others – whether they are sufficiently thought of, whether well enough nursed, whether visited often enough. How much time is thus devoted to considering the body and what it needs, rather than to the Lord and the relationship which he seeks to establish with their souls. Oh, how many are they who, through sickness, are occupied almost exclusively with themselves! All this is totally different when healing is sought for in faith from the loving God. Then the first thing to learn is to cease to be anxious about the state of your body. You have trusted it to the Lord, and he has taken the responsibility.[4]

References

1. Harper M., *Jesus the Healer*, Highland, 1986.

2. Rawcliffe C., p.14,15, *Medicine and Society in Later Medieval England*, Alan Sutton, 1995. I am indebted to Rawcliffe for these medieval beliefs.

3. Thomas A Kempis, p.68, *The Imitation of Christ*, Collins, 1957.

4. Murray A. p.53, *Divine Healing*, Whitaker House, 1982.

Chapter 6

FORGIVEN!

If he has sinned he will be forgiven.

James is saying here that sin may be the cause of illness. There was a widespread belief in Bible times that an illness was caused by sin either committed by the sufferer or even by his or her parents (John 9:2).

Out of all the illnesses that Jesus healed, in only two do we read that sin was the cause. One was the paralysed man let down through the roof by his friends (Mark 2:1-12). When Jesus saw him he said, 'Son, your sins are forgiven.' Jesus then confirmed he had the right to forgive sins, implying he was God, by telling him to get up and go home. He healed him of his sin and his sickness. There is a striking similarity between this account and our passage in James. The man's friends are like the elders. With his agreement or even perhaps at his request, they brought him to Jesus; the elders bring the sick person to Jesus in prayer. The friends had the faith to do it, even to overcome obstacles. It was action in faith; James has the prayer in faith. The man's sins were forgiven and he was healed; in James the sick one is healed and his sins, if any, are forgiven. Jesus forgave, which could not be seen and could have been blasphemous, and then proved he was God and not blaspheming, by healing. The forgiveness was the greater miracle and this is still true today.

The other example of sin and healing was the man at the pool of Bethesda (John 5:1-15). Jesus healed the man and later told him to stop sinning in case something worse happened to him. It is interesting that Jesus healed first and then confronted him about his sin. Is this an example of someone being healed who was not a child of God? We do not know.

Still today, when illness strikes, people say, 'What have I done to deserve this?' or 'I have lived a good life, why has this happened to me?' Now illness can be our own fault. If we abuse our bodies by smoking, drinking too much alcohol or eating too much, can we really complain if disease occurs? Is that sin?

Let us suppose that a Christian has lung cancer. He smoked, so his smoking caused the illness. There is no excuse for anybody now not knowing that smoking is harmful and that it abuses the body. Even King James in the seventeenth century knew that smoking was dangerous for the lungs![1] So we could argue that smoking is sin. Is that what James means? I do not for a moment think that only smokers are more sinful than others. Smokers and non-smokers are alike in need of the saving grace of the Lord Jesus. I feel strongly about smoking because I see the damage it causes. I do feel sorry for people with lung cancer and try to help them as much as those with a sexually transmitted disease or a little innocent child with appendicitis. I, as a doctor, may know the state of the body but only God knows the state of their soul. A surgeon may penetrate skin and organs with scalpels and needles, but God penetrates to divide soul and spirit, even to the very centre of our beings by his Word (Heb. 4:12).

In most illnesses, there is not such a clear cause and effect as in lung cancer. So I do not think James means that sin is ignorance or carelessness about health risks.

What does James mean by sin?

James wrote to Christians. A Christian is dead to sin and therefore sin does not have any hold on him or her (Rom. 6:1-2). The consequence of our sinful nature, eternal or spiritual death, has been removed. We do not need to sin because we have a new nature. We are still troubled by our old nature and so can be tripped up and commit a sin. 'Anyone, then, who knows the good he ought to do and does not do it, sins' (James 4:17). Our old nature is in conflict with the Spirit because they desire different things (Gal. 5:17).

Sin is the breaking of God's laws and knowing that the law has been broken. The word for 'sinned' in James 5:15 is *hamartia*, meaning intentional sin associated with guilt. The same word is used in James 4:17. If in a certain circumstance, we know by our actions we have not loved God with all our hearts, or have not loved another as ourselves, then we have sinned. A Christian cannot continue in sin and not know about it because the Holy Spirit dwells in us. He speaks to our conscience: 'God is my witness' (Rom. 1:9); 'my own conscience enlightened by the Holy Spirit' (Rom. 9:1, NEB). When he convicts our conscience about sin, if we confess that sin and repent of it, then we will be forgiven and cleansed.

According to one book[2], the construction of the sentence, 'if he has sinned he will be forgiven', implies a past act of which the effect remains. The author paraphrased it as: 'If he is in the state of having committed sins, the effect of which remains, he will be forgiven.' Obviously a serious problem.

The problem comes if we do not repent or if we continue in the sin. Our heavenly Father will not leave us in that state because 'no-one who is born of God will continue to sin (*hamartia*), because God's seed remains in him; he cannot go on sinning, because he has been born of God' (1 John 3:9). Therefore he 'will discipline those he loves, and punish everyone he accepts as a son' (Heb. 12:6). '... God disciplines us for our good, that we may share in his holiness ... discipline produces a harvest of righteousness and peace' (Heb. 12:10, 11).

The Father's Correction

What is God's discipline? There may be a number of things that God uses such as disappointments or friends letting us down. It may simply be that we lose our joy or that Bible study and prayer seem difficult. God's discipline may also be illness. In Hebrews we read that the Father will punish everyone he accepts as a son. In fact, it is a sign of being a child of God (Heb. 12:6 ff.). 'Punish' or 'scourge' is the same word that is used for 'diseases' in Mark

3:10; 'suffering illness' in Mark 5:29 and 34; and 'sicknesses' in Luke 7:21. It must be said that on none of these occasions are we told that sin was the cause of the illness. Paul told the Corinthians that many of them were sick or even had died because they had sinned at the Lord's Supper (1 Cor. 11:30). The sin was that they had not recognised or judged correctly the Lord's body. They had taken lightly the bread and wine, even considering the sacrament as an ordinary meal to satisfy hunger. The meaning may also be that they judged each other incorrectly. There were divisions or factions or cliques. They were not in unity, not together. They had something against each other and so did not recognise the group of believers as the Lord's body and therefore holy. Jesus told us not to judge other people, for if we do we will be judged by the same standards (Matt. 7:1). Paul assured the Corinthians that if they corrected themselves, they would not be disciplined by God, and surely that is for us too. God may send illness to correct us because he loves us (Rev. 3:19). The important thing is to accept the discipline of the Lord (Psalm 119:75).

I think, therefore, this message of James implied in verse 15 is: a Christian has sinned, has disobeyed a clear command in God's Word. He knows he has sinned but does not repent. Indeed he continues to do the wrong thing. It is a very definite disobedience, not just carelessness about health matters. His Father, God, loves him as a son and does not want to condemn him with the world (1 Cor. 11:32), so he disciplines him by sending an illness. By asking the church for prayer the Christian is saying he accepts God's rebuke, repents and receives forgiveness and healing. I think I am right in suggesting that if the illness is a discipline sent by God for sin, if that sin is confessed and prayer is made, God will heal. He will cure miraculously or through medicine. If the sin is not confessed, then the person may continue to suffer from the illness and may even die, but will still be saved for eternity because he is a son and nothing will separate him from his Father. However, we must heed the warning about sinning against the fellowship in Hebrews 10:25ff. I would like to emphasise that the sin is known to the Christian, the Holy Spirit makes sure of that. There is no need for the sick to search for unknown sins which do not exist (Psalm 32:3-5).

Finally, in this painful section, a positive, joyful note. The word 'forgiven' in James 5:15 means to send away or remit. 'It means the removal of the punishment and it removes the cause of the offence because it is based on the sacrifice of the Lord Jesus Christ for our sins.'[3] Praise God! Psalm 103:12 promises that our sins are removed as far as the east is from the west and, Paul writes that we have forgiveness of our sins according to the grace of God which is lavished on us with wisdom and understanding (Eph. 1:7, 8). I am thrilled by that last bit – the Lord does understand.

Most illness is not a punishment for sin

Other Christians do not know if the sick one has sinned and it is very dangerous for them to accuse the sick one of sin when none exists. It is possible that God may reveal to us that sickness in others is caused by sin, but we must be so careful. We do not possess the diagnostic skills of the Great Physician, our Lord Jesus.[4] The sick one's conscience may also be at fault, accusing of wrong doing when there is no such thing. This is especially prevalent in depression, where the sufferer may think he is guilty of all sorts of imaginary things. John reminds us that God is greater than our hearts (conscience) and he knows everything (1 John 3:18-20). It is very important for the elders to reassure the innocent sick that the illness is not their fault. As a doctor I find I have to do this often. It is a lovely thing to be able to do.

Jesus confirmed that sickness may not be the result of sin. His disciples asked him if the blind man or his parents had sinned? Jesus said neither (John 9:2-3). James says about the sick one that 'if he has sinned he will be forgiven.' The 'if' is important. Job is a good example. He had not sinned and yet his friends tried to make him agree that he had. They were censured by God which is a lesson for us all.

There are many examples in the Bible of sickness not being due to sin. I will simply list them:

1. Moses' leprous arm (Exodus 4:6).
2. Job's sores.
3. Man born blind (John 9:1).
4. Lazarus (John 11:2).
5. Paul's blindness (Acts 9:8).
6. Dorcas (Acts 9:37).
7. Jesus himself – weakness (2 Cor. 13:4).
8. By implication in James – 'IF'.

In most other sicknesses in the Bible, as forgiveness is not mentioned, I think we are safe to assume that sin was not an issue. These include the great majority of the people healed by Jesus; those healed in Acts; Paul himself (1 Cor. 2:3; 2 Cor. 12:9; Gal. 4:13); and Epaphroditus (Phil. 2:27).

I believe that most illness is not a judgement or discipline by God. If all illness was sent by God for correction, then it would be wrong to be a doctor. In the Middle Ages, if a doctor was treating a person who refused to confess his sin, if he continued to treat the sick one, the doctor was at risk of excommunication. This was because the church organisation believed all illness was a punishment sent by God, so the doctor was fighting against God. The Lord Jesus himself has shown us that not all illness is sent by God. The elders, in responding to the call, should treat the sick one as innocent, unless the sick one tells them otherwise. There must also be objective evidence of that sin, in case his conscience is wrongly condemning him.

Rest in his Love

So, if illness develops, the Bible's teaching is that we should examine ourselves to see if we have *unrepented* sin. If so we should confess it to God, repent and ask his forgiveness. If God does not reveal any sin to us, or if there is sin and we receive his forgiveness we should forget it. He has! We should then rest in his love, we know him, and his law is written on our hearts (Jer.

31:33, 34). It is unnecessary to continue agonising, trying desperately to find a hidden sin. I know that we sin every day which is why we need daily private communion with our God. What does Jesus say? 'Here I am! I stand at the door and knock. If anyone hears my voice and opens the door, I will come in and eat with him, and he with me' (Rev. 3:20). He is talking about repentance, but this verse is a lovely picture of perfect health, wholeness of body, mind and spirit. The Lord sharing a meal with me. I am reminded of the original scene in Eden, where God walked with man in the cool of the evening. Praise God, this will occur again.

Conclusion

The elders should have a time of quietness with the sick person so that all present may be able to confess any sins to God. It may be that the sick one will want to confess something to the group but I do not think it is essential. What a reassurance that God accepts us as we are. Let us remind ourselves of the promise, 'he will be forgiven', and 'if we confess our sins, he is faithful and just and will forgive us our sins', whatever they are.

References

1. Burke J., p.122, *An Illustrated History of England*, Book Club Associates, 1974.

2. John J., p.56, in *The Oil of Gladness*, Ed. Dudley M. & Rowell G., SPCK, 1993.

3. Vine's *Complete Expository Dictionary of Old and New Testament Words*, p.250, Vine W.E., Unger M.F., & White W. Jr., Thomas Nelson, 1985.

4. Campbell Morgan G., *The Great Physician*, Marshall, Morgan & Scott, 1937.

Chapter 7

OUR DUTY TO EACH OTHER

Confess your sins to each other and pray for each other so that you may be healed. The prayer of a righteous man is powerful and effective.

James turns from the special or particular prayer of the elders for the sick person to our prayers for each other. He is still thinking about prayer for healing but advises us to pray for or, rather, to continue in prayer for each other. The Greek tenses show that the prayer of the elders was one definite act, but here prayer is continuous. Of course, the elders can be asked to pray again, and should pray again if there is a change in the condition such as an impending operation. Let us look at examples of continuous prayer by believers for others in the Bible.

Intercessory Prayer

Moses interceded for the people of Israel when they had worshipped the golden calf (Exod. 32:32). He asked God to forgive them even to the extent of putting his own salvation on the line.

Our Lord Jesus prayed for all believers and asked his Father that we all may be in unity (John 17:20, 21). He intercedes for us at this very moment with the Father (Heb. 7:25), on the grounds that he died bearing our sin (Isa. 53:12), and now lives for ever.

Paul was always praying for the Christians he knew. He told the Romans, Thessalonians and Timothy that they were constantly in his prayers. He prayed that the Ephesians would be strengthened with power and filled with all the fulness of God. He continued to pray that they would know God better (Eph. 1:15-23; 3:14-21). For the Philippians he prayed that their love would abound more and more in knowledge and depth of insight (Phil. 1:9), and for the Colossians that they would be filled with the knowledge of God's will (Col. 1:9). We have already seen the importance of love, knowledge and insight given by God as we pray for the sick. Paul prayed that Philemon would be active in sharing his faith (Phil. 6). He advised his readers to copy him, praying on all occasions with all kinds of prayers and requests (Eph. 6:18).

John was also very concerned about his Christian friends, calling them his children. For an elder called Gaius he prayed that he would enjoy good health, even as his soul was getting along well (3 John 2).

From these examples we can see how important it is to keep on praying. I have already quoted part of Ephesians 6, it goes on: 'Be alert and always keep on praying for all the saints.' We are told to pray continually (1 Thess. 5:17), and to be faithful in prayer (Rom. 12:11). When we are anxious about anything – perhaps for someone who is ill – we are told to bring our requests to God, by prayer and petition, with thanksgiving (Phil. 4:6). We are to pray even when we do not know how to pray or what to pray for. Then the Holy Spirit himself will intercede for us (Rom. 8:26). For a Christian, it should be as natural as breathing to pray to the heavenly Father. It is noteworthy that prayer or intercession is not included in the lists of the gifts of the Spirit (Rom. 12:6-8; 1 Cor. 12:4-10, 28-31; Eph. 4:11-13; 1 Peter 4:10-11). We do not need a special gift of praying; we are children of God, a child does not need special abilities to speak to his father. Because of our great High Priest, the Lord Jesus, we can approach God at the throne of grace with confidence, so finding the mercy and grace that we need (Heb. 4:16).

The Cost of Prayer

It is apparent from the examples above that praying is a very privileged and joyous experience, but it is also very costly in time and effort. We have already noted that for Jesus to be able to pray or intercede for us, the transgressors, he had to suffer and die for us. Norman Grubb, in *Rees Howells Intercessor*[1], stated that there were three things found in an intercessor: identification, agony and authority. We certainly find these in Jesus: he identified with us in our sin; he went through agony on the cross; and he now lives having been given all authority. We see this in Philippians 2: *identification* in verse 7 – Jesus was 'made in human likeness'; *agony* in verse 8 – 'he was obedient to death'; and *authority* in verse 10 – 'at the name of Jesus every knee should bow.' We are called to follow our Lord: 'each of you should look not only to your own interests but also to the interests of others. Your attitude should be the same as that of Christ Jesus' (Phil. 2:4-5). Rees Howells believed he was asked by the Holy Spirit to go to great lengths to identify with the people he interceded for. With one woman who had consumption (tuberculosis), he was challenged to die in her place so her children would be looked after. Ultimately he was not asked to pay that price but the point is, he was willing to.

When we pray for others we are to share the suffering. When we turn to our passage in James and see that we are to keep on praying for each other, we see some of the cost and, yes, agony involved. It is very painful to admit we are in the wrong. We are to confess our sins to each other. This literally means we are to agree together, in the sight of God, our faults and our shortcomings. This means saying sorry. This means, in humility, considering other people better than ourselves. I don't think this means telling each other our darkest secrets, these are between us and God. It means any fault that is affecting our fellowship with other Christians, especially when we know that they have been hurt by the shortcoming. James uses a different word here for sin* – *paraptoma* – than he does in the preceding verse, perhaps meaning faults in our relations with other people as opposed to sins only against God. He means unintentional sin, being tripped up, the

---

*Not all Greek manuscripts agree that it is a different word – some use the same word, *hamartia*. It seems to me that the NKJV is correct in using different words: sins and trespasses respectively,

hasty word. Note too that this is a two-way traffic: confess *to each other* and pray *for each other*. Of necessity this also means forgiving each other. The Lord has forgiven, we also should forgive.

> 'Bear with each other (or put up with each other), and forgive whatever grievances you may have against one another. Forgive as the Lord forgave you. And over all these virtues put on love' (Col. 3:13, 14).

Word for word, the meaning is: forgive yourselves if anyone against anyone should have a complaint.[2] Why? Because in Christ we are one body, at peace, in unity. So, as we are honest and open with each other in love, we can pray for healing. I am not sure how significant it is that the words are 'may be healed' rather than 'will be healed' (James 5:16). All I can say is that healing is according to the will of God. The important point is that we may not expect healing if we have unresolved grievances with each other.

The final characteristic of an intercessor is authority – authority given by God. Rees Howells had authority. So did George Müller. Is it not wonderful how in our own time, certain Christians speak with quiet authority? I can think of godly people I know who have authority.

Healing – *iaomai*

Looking back to James 5:15, we remember that the word for 'make well' or 'heal' was *sozo* which also means 'save'. Here in verse 16 the word for 'healed' is different, it is *iaomai* which usually means physical healing but can include spiritual healing (1 Peter 2:24). It may mean that James is thinking of healing in the widest sense – physical healing, healing of rifts between two Christians, and healing of a broken heart. He could have used *therapeuo* which means medical care. Anyway this healing comes about by praying for each other in love, not allowing anything to separate us.

Righteous, not self-righteous

James goes on: 'The prayer of a righteous man is powerful and effective.' At first this is a bit off-putting. We think our prayers cannot be effective because we are not good enough. There is still a lot in our lives that is not right. We may feel the same way when we read our Lord's words: 'Be perfect, therefore, as your heavenly Father is perfect' (Matt. 5:48). The devil is so good at tripping us up. If we think we are not good enough then we will not pray earnestly for these great blessings. We need to remind ourselves that it is not our goodness or righteousness which makes us worthy, it is Christ's. We are clothed in his righteousness. Because we have faith in him this is credited to us as righteousness (Rom. 4:5, 24). There is a very clear passage in John's first letter which I would like to quote in full :

> 'But if we walk in the light, as he is in the light, we have fellowship with one another, and the blood of Jesus, his Son, purifies us from all sin. If we claim to be without sin, we deceive ourselves and the truth is not in us. If we confess our sins he is faithful and just to forgive us our sins and purify us from all unrighteousness' (1 John 1:7-9).

If we have been purified from all unrighteousness that means we are righteous, but only as we walk in his light and do not try to keep sins hidden. We saw previously that Jesus had to die before he could intercede for us. Praise God, he rose again to put us right before God (Rom. 4:25). We have to die to self in a very real sense to truly pray and intercede for each other. First of all, we need to realise that, as Christians, we have been born again. As far as our position before God stands our old natures are indeed dead, we have new life. This is not our doing, this is one of the miracles of God's grace. We just need to accept it. What we have to do is to get rid of the remaining parts of the old nature that stop our new life being effective in prayer. It is thrilling how so often God's grace to us and encouragement for our efforts are interwoven in the Bible. His *grace* and our *effort* are entwined together; you cannot have one without the other. Robert Dale said that by grace, 'that which God asks for he gives .... Every precept is but the reverse of a promise; every command is but the prophecy of a grace'.[3] There is a good example in Paul's letter to the Colossians, chapter 3. We have been raised with Christ [*grace*]; set your hearts and minds on things above [*effort*]; you died, and your life is hidden with Christ in God [*grace*]; put to death what belongs to your earthly nature [*effort*]. There follows a list of things we should get rid of: sexual sins, greed, anger, slander, lies and so on. Then it is *grace* again, as we try to do these things, our new self is being renewed in knowledge by the Holy Spirit. As it happens, in my Bible, I have to turn over a new leaf to find what we should aim for: compassion, kindness, gentleness, forgiveness and above all love, doing all in the name of the Lord Jesus (Col. 3:1-17).

Power Praying

'The prayer of a righteous man is powerful and effective.' In other words, the prayer of a man (or woman) who is right with God, and walking in the Spirit, is full of the energy or power of the Spirit and is very effective. We could say such a prayer has authority. A possible meaning of the Greek is: 'the energy filled prayer of the righteous man produces energy.' The amazing fact is that our prayers release the incredible power and energy of Almighty God.

At school we learnt about energy. The law of conservation of energy states that energy cannot be created or destroyed. It can be changed from one form into another. For example, the potential energy in coal can be changed into heat and light. The energy in the coal came from sunlight acting on plants millions of years before. The light energy from the sun was changed into chemical energy in the plants as they grew. When the plants died, this energy was stored. Ultimately, all the energy on the earth comes from the sun and the sun's energy is produced by nuclear fusion reaction.

This discussion about energy is a good illustration of the power of prayer. The potential energy that God has is unlimited. He created it. This energy cannot be lost. Prayer is the way God has designed for his energy to be used: energy or power for salvation, healing, and sanctification. We have unlimited power on tap. 'My word will not return unto me empty,' says God, 'but will accomplish what I desire and achieve the purpose for which I sent it' (Isa. 55:11). 'Word' has a very wide meaning in the Bible. Not only does it mean something spoken, but it can also mean the action that is spoken about. For example, Psalm 107:20: 'He sent his word, and healed them.' In John 1, Jesus himself is the Word. So if we pray in the Spirit we can be assured that our prayer is heard, that it will be answered and that it will do what God has intended.

Surely all this will encourage us to pray. James gives the example of Elijah. The point James was making is that Elijah was an ordinary man, just like you or me (James 5:17,18); yet great miracles occurred in answer to his prayers. We read that he prayed earnestly. The Greek says 'he prayed a prayer', the double word emphasising how fervent his prayer was. How was he so sure that his prayers would be answered? Because God had revealed it to him. We read; 'As the LORD, the God of Israel, lives, whom I serve' (1 Kings 17:1). Elijah was saying that he was obeying a command from the living God. We can pray like that, releasing the power of God as we obey him.

References

1. Grubb N., *Rees Howells Intercessor*, Lutterworth Press, 1952.

2. Colossians 3:13. *The NKJV Greek English Interlinear New Testament*, Farstad A.L., Hodges Z.C., Moss C.M., Picirilli R.E., & Pickering W.N., Thomas Nelson, 1994.

3. Dale R.W., p .136, *The Epistle of James*, 1895, quoted in *Evangelical Spirituality*, by Gordon J.M., p.154, SPCK, 1991.

Chapter 8

SPECIAL GIFTS

I want now to consider some other topics which have an important bearing on healing. The first of these is the gifts of the Spirit.

Gifts are given by the Holy Spirit for the good of the church. Obviously the Spirit can and does give whatever gifts he desires, so the lists that we are given in the Bible are possibly not exhaustive. The lists of gifts that he does give to his church are found in 1 Corinthians 12, Romans 12, Ephesians 4 and 1 Peter 4. The gifts are apostles, prophets and prophecy, teachers, miracles, healing, helpers or deeds of helping, administrators or organisation, tongues, interpreters of tongues, wisdom, knowledge, faith, discerning spirits, evangelists, pastors, leaders, preachers, encouragers, serving, giving and being merciful. The gifts are given for the common good (1 Cor. 12:7), and to build up the church (Eph. 4:12). It is interesting that it says, for example, 'giving' or 'contributing' rather than 'givers' or 'contributers'. We are all called to give of our time and money but sometimes they are gifts of the Spirit and so a great privilege and joy to be able to give more. The same applies to healing: it is a gift of healing and not of healers.

In the passages mentioned there are slightly different emphases. In 1 Corinthians 12, Romans 12 and 1 Peter 4, the emphasis is that the gifts are given to individuals; while in Ephesians 4 and in a list at the end of 1 Corinthians 12 the emphasis is on gifts to the church. For example the gift of apostleship was not given to a man; apostles were chosen by the Lord Jesus and given to the church.

There are I think four gifts that are directly concerned with the Church's ministry of healing: the gifts of healing, wisdom, knowledge and faith. These gifts are all mentioned in 1 Corinthians, but are not mentioned in the other accounts. Incidentally, James does mention them. He says we should ask God for wisdom (1:5), and he also has a lot to say about faith, especially that faith without deeds is dead (2:26), meaning that we should help people in material ways as well as praying for them. We have already seen that the prayer in faith (James 5:15) implies having the gifts of knowledge and faith. These gifts, together with miraculous powers, speaking and interpretation of tongues, are spectacular. The other gifts, such as prophecy, leadership, teaching, encouraging, giving, serving, and so on, have been called ordinary gifts and are found in the other passages and are more likely to be found in most churches. It is wrong to call them ordinary gifts because down the ages they have been the means of great blessing to the church. I should perhaps add that prophecy is not so much new revelations as it is speaking the word of God that he has given for that church for that day. Our ministers and clergy should be doing that, and often are every Sunday. So when the preacher announces the word that the Lord 'has laid on my heart', he is exercising a gift of the Spirit. In fact Paul wrote 'eagerly desire spiritual gifts, especially the gift of prophecy' (1 Cor. 14:1), so that the listeners are strengthened, encouraged and comforted.

Are all these gifts for us?

The question then arises: as these spectacular gifts are only mentioned in 1 Corinthians, were they given only for that group of believers? Wonderful instances of healing and other miracles are recorded in the Book of Acts, in places other than Corinth, but they usually involved one of the apostles, the exceptions being Stephen (Acts 6:8) and Philip (Acts 8:7). Paul asked the Galatians, whether it was their faith that caused God to give them his Spirit and work miracles among them (Gal. 3:5). Obviously the answer was 'yes'. This shows that miracles occurred in Galatia. These miracles could, however, have happened when Paul was there, or they may have been the miracle of changed lives. The writer of

Hebrews, in warning against ignoring the great salvation through Christ, mentioned that God testified to salvation by means of signs, wonders, miracles and gifts of the Spirit (Heb. 2:4). In the NIV 'testified' is in the past tense, suggesting that such manifestations of God's power were over. I understand, however, that the tense of 'testify' is present, suggesting that such things were still happening at least when Hebrews was written (see AV, NKJV and REB). Peter, John, and Jude do not mention the spectacular gifts. The second letter to the Corinthians was probably written only a few months after the first, but in it Paul hardly mentioned such gifts. When he did mention signs, wonders and miracles, he said they were the mark of an apostle (2 Cor. 12:12), meaning that if they had not occurred, he could not be an apostle. This is not the same as saying that such things only happened when an apostle was present. Paul was defending his position.

Jesus, in talking to the eleven disciples or apostles, after his resurrection, promised:

'these signs will accompany those who believe: In my name they [so not the disciples present] will drive out demons; they will speak in new tongues; they will pick up snakes ... and drink deadly poison, (which) will not hurt them; they will place their hands on sick people and they will get well' (Mark 16:17, 18).

There were two apostles added later, Matthias and Paul, but it is stretching it a bit to say that these promises were limited to those two. This passage is from the 'long ending of Mark', and it is not certain if it is genuine. However, if it was added later in the third century, the author was presumably writing about what was known to have happened. Whether they were Jesus' words or not, we have to say that the spectacular gifts did occur in groups other and as well as the Corinthians. All such gifts are the work of the Spirit and only he decides who to give them to (1 Cor. 12:11).

Gifts are not a measure of holiness or maturity

Although a church may have many gifts of healing or tongues, this
does not mean that the members are more spiritual or that they
love the Lord more. Indeed the Corinthians were rebuked by Paul
more than any other church! What did he say to them that is recorded
for us? 'I always thank God for you because of his grace ... you
have been enriched in him in every way .... Therefore you do not
lack any spiritual gift' (1 Cor. 1:4, 5, 7). Wonderful, what a Spirit-
filled church, we would say. But, two chapters later, we read:
'You are still worldly, since there is jealousy and quarrelling among
you' (3:3). The Corinthians had received the gifts of the Spirit;
but they were not producing the fruit of the Spirit (Gal. 5:22). The
gifts of the Spirit are given by grace to build up the church, they
do not depend on how mature we are as Christians. Pride, therefore,
has no place but is a danger. If we are blessed by gifts, we need to
produce fruit. This is why Paul showed the Corinthians the most
excellent way of love in 1 Corinthians 13; and why James insisted
that faith is dead if there is no action: 'As the body without the
spirit is dead, so faith without deeds is dead' (James 2:26). Perhaps
I could paraphrase this: 'The local church, the body of Christ,
will not survive without the Spirit, but when he is present he will
produce gifts and deeds of love.'

Gifts in his name

Some have said that the spectacular or miracle gifts ceased after
the time of the apostles. We have no authority to say this. The so
called Charismatic Movement, starting in the Pentecostal churches
and spreading to many other denominations, shows that the Holy
Spirit is continuing to give these gifts for the building up of the
church. However, we should remember that the use of such gifts
should be 'in his name', and that means sometimes, according to
his will, they will not be used. We cannot presume that the gift
will be given. The giving is the sole prerogative of the Holy Spirit,
although we are encouraged to ask for them (1 Cor. 14:1). We
should also humbly realise that the gifts did not stop until the late

nineteenth century. Francis MacNutt said that it is probably easier for Catholics to accept the present day miracles because they have been used to them.[1] Lourdes is a good example. The Catholic Church has venerated people who have been involved in miraculous healings down the centuries. One of the requirements for canonisation, calling somebody a 'saint', is evidence of such healings being associated with them. Some of the stories of the saints are just legends and there are only very few truly attested miracles from Lourdes but some, perhaps most, of the stories of healing from the past have some truth. If so, these people, the 'saints', were demonstrating a gift of the Spirit.

For examples of healings through the Holy Spirit in the past, I would recommend the books by Gardner, Gunstone and Wimber.[2] These books also detail more recent healings.

Are gifts genuine?

One of the problems is that there can be counterfeit gifts produced by Satan. We are told that he can appear as an angel of light (2 Cor. 11:14). Jesus warned us that before he comes again with power and great glory, false Christs and false prophets will perform great signs and miracles, so much so that even the elect, the church of God, will find them difficult to explain (Matt. 24:24). Herbert Carson points out that the devil would not mind if people had good health through his miracles as long as they were lost for eternity.[3] Paul therefore gave clear teaching to the Corinthians in this twelfth chapter of his first letter to them.

Paul reminded the Corinthians that, before they became Christians, they were led astray; he advised them and us how to discern if gifts of miracles, including healing, are genuine. It all depends on the attitude to the Lord Jesus. No one curses Jesus if they are speaking by the Spirit of God; and no one admits that Jesus is their Lord unless the Holy Spirit is working in their lives. These two things go together to prove that the gift is genuine; one, the absence of blaspheming the Lord and two, the owning of the Lordship of Christ. I suppose it is just possible, with much squirming, for a demon to say and pretend that Jesus is Lord; but I am sure that any Christian would agree that they would find it impossible to let the words 'Jesus be cursed' escape from their lips. Quite spectacular healings have been claimed in New Age circles and some doctors are using eastern mysticism, but if the Lordship of Christ is not acknowledged, such activities are ultimately of no benefit. By 'genuine', I mean by the Spirit of God, not genuine in the sense of being true miracles. The devil can produce true wonders. It is also necessary to say that true Christians can believe a miracle has occurred, when there has been a natural phenomenon. This, of course, could still have been a gift of the Spirit, if the name of the Lord Jesus is glorified. The Bible goes on to say that the gifts are given for the common good (1 Cor. 12:7); to build up the church (1 Cor. 14:12; Eph. 4:12); to prepare God's people for works of service (Eph. 4:12); so that in all things God may be praised through Jesus Christ (1 Pet. 4:11). That is too tall an order for any counterfeit gift! Jesus also said that we will recognise false prophets by their fruit, by the results (Matt. 7:20). Note the awful warning he gave to those who prophesy or perform miracles, pretending to be in his name, but do not know him as Lord and Saviour (Matt. 7:22, 23). Obedience to the revealed will of God in the Bible is so important.

To build up the church

The fruit or results of the gifts of the Spirit are not, then, the immediate effects. The eternally important effect of a gift of healing is not the healing but the effect the healing has on the church. That is a very important point. Miraculous healing of serious or chronic disease, in answer to our prayers, will only be granted if it builds up the church for service and the common good, so that God is praised. We see now why the cure of serious illness may not occur. God does not do the sensational just because it is sensational. Jesus had this problem, which is one possible reason why, on at least six occasions,[4] he asked people to keep quiet about his miracles. When a miracle or cure was used to demonstrate his power to a crowd or to the Jewish leaders, the deed was done openly. We have details of eight healing miracles performed by the Lord in or near Jerusalem. None were done secretly. Five appeared to be planned in that Jesus sought out the sick people and in healing them, he demonstrated some point to the Jews. These points were: he could forgive sin; he came from God; he could raise the dead, proving that God had sent him; and to show that rules such as the Sabbath were not important in the face of real need (twice). The other three simply happened because Jesus had compassion, but they were done openly. In Galilee and the surrounding area the cure was often done secretly, Jesus responded in compassion to a need. He often led people aside or went into a house. In Galilee, only three recorded healings were done as a special witness, while six were done quietly out of compassion. Five out of these six were warned not to tell others, although not all obeyed. Once, a group who were healed were warned not to say who he was. This was to show that Jesus was going to bring justice and peace to the nations in a quiet, unexciting way. He was not going to hurt humble, ordinary people. It pleases God that people come to him through preaching rather than miraculous signs (1 Cor. 1:21, 22). However, because our God is full of compassion, he may heal miraculously when we least expect it. Why he does not do this often we must leave to his infinite love and wisdom. He does know best.

What is the fruit of the Spirit? Love, joy, peace, patience, kindness, goodness, faithfulness, gentleness and self-control (Gal. 5:22). What a lovely picture of what the Spirit is doing in our lives which will be made perfect in heaven.

In 1 Corinthians 12, Paul also brings out a wonderful picture of the three Persons of the Godhead working together. The various gifts are given by the Spirit, to serve the Lord Jesus in different ways, so that God works all of them in all men (verses 4-6). There are different gifts, different men and women receiving those gifts; yet the same Spirit, same Lord, and same God. Paul is reminding us that although there is a great variety of work that God accomplishes through giving gifts to his people, yet there is unity in God – the doctrine of the Trinity.

In the next chapter, the gifts of healing, wisdom, knowledge and faith will be considered as they apply to the Church's ministry of healing.

References

1. MacNutt F., p.13, *Healing*, Fowler Wright Books Ltd., 1974.

2. Gardner R., *Healing Miracles*, Darton, Longman and Todd, 1986; Gunstone J., *The Lord is our Healer*, Hodder and Stoughton, 1986; Wimber J. & Springer K., *Power Healing*, Hodder and Stoughton, 1986.

3. Carson H., *Spiritual Gifts for Today*, p. 93, Kingsway, 1987.

4. These were: a man with leprosy (Mark 1:44); Jairus' daughter (Mark 5:43); a deaf and dumb man (Mark 7:36); a blind man (Mark 8:26); two blind men (Matt. 9:30) and a group (Luke 17:14).

Chapter 9

THE GIFTS OF HEALINGS NOT HEALERS

To one there is given through the Spirit the message of wisdom, to another the message of knowledge by means of the same Spirit, to another faith by the same Spirit, to another gifts of healing by that one Spirit (1 Cor. 12: 8, 9).

I believe when there is a need in the body of Christ, the local church, the Spirit is ready to give the necessary gifts to his people to relieve that need. We remind ourselves that gifts from the Spirit will be in the name of the Lord, in God's will. We are thinking of illness in one of the members of the body. If it will benefit the whole church, the Spirit may give the gift of miraculous healing, literally, the gift of a cure. We have already come across the word *iaomai* which is the verb 'to heal'. Now we have the word *iama*, a noun, 'a cure', the effect of healing. Note it is the gift of a cure, not the ability to cure. People may say that someone has the gift of healing but the passage suggests that the gift is to the person who is healed and not to the person who prays for him or her. Last Christmas I gave my son the gift of a computer game, the gift was to him and for him, it was not for me to use for him. I was glad about that, I'm hopeless at computer games! This is a simple illustration but it makes the point.

There are, in fact, two related Greek words translated by the English nouns 'healing' and 'cures' in the New Testament. One is *iama* (actually *iamaton* – plural) used only in 1 Corinthians 12. The other is *iasis*, used three times by Luke. The uses by Luke are: (1) Jesus said, 'I ... perform cures today ...' (Luke 13:32); (2) Acts 4: 22: 'on whom this miracle of healing had been performed'; and (3) Acts 4: 30: 'Stretch out your (the Lord) hand to heal (lit. for healing). Strong differentiates the two words as follows: *iama* is the effect of healing, while *iasis* is the act of healing. According to Dr G. Cockburn, *iama* is a cure while *iasis* is the more abstract process of healing although the distinction may not always have been followed.[1] He said that *charismata iamaton* (in Corinthians) really means gifts in the form of cures. I think this strongly suggests that the gift of healing, that is the effect or result of healing, is given to the sick one and not to a healer, when it would have been the act of healing.

I simplified things a little above by talking about the gift of healing. It is actually plural, the gifts of healings or the gifts of cures. I should say, here, that nearly all commentaries I have read suggest that the gift is to cure, or the ability to cure. In fact, the Good News Bible translates this as 'to another person he gives the power to heal.' The Living Bible is similar. The problem is that 'power' does not occur in the Greek. 'Power' is a commonly used word in the Bible, the Greek word is *dunamis* from which we get our word 'dynamite'. The plural of this word is, in fact, used in the next phrase: miraculous powers or *dunameis* (1 Cor. 12:9). Most versions use the words as in the NIV: 'to another the gifts of healing(s)'; and this does appear to be the correct translation. When you think about it, I believe you will agree that 'gifts of healings' are to the person healed or possibly to the church, rather than to one person who has some special skill in healing. David Watson said, 'The gift of healing is not owned by a person, but is given to the one who is sick.'[2] I think he meant that the gift is given by God to the one who is sick, rather than through an intermediary. The latter just does not sound right. After all it is God who heals. Jesus we are told went about healing the sick and he sent out his disciples to heal the sick (Matt. 10:8). The word here, however, is different (*therapeuo*) and could mean give service and help to the sick (cf. served – Acts 17:25; servants, *therapeia* – Luke 12:42), although in some situations its use was in the miraculous (e.g. Matt. 15:30). Anyway, the disciples were in a special situation. *Iaomai* is rarely used in the healing of crowds and only by Luke the doctor; presumably to emphasise the miraculous. Luke has an interesting phrase: 'and (he) healed (*iato* from *iama*) those who needed healing *(therapeuo)*' (Luke 9:11). I think this could be rendered: 'and he cured (miraculously) those who needed medical care.'

In Jesus' words to the disciples before his ascension, he did not command them to heal the sick, he promised that the sick would get well (Mark 16:18). In the more usual situation of the church in Acts, after Pentecost, we are only once told that an apostle healed somebody (Acts 28:8); but we are often told the sick were healed by the power of the Holy Spirit or in the name of Jesus. All the letters in the New Testament are full of instructions to do things, but in them we are never told to go and heal. This statement can be criticised in that it is an argument from silence, there are plenty of suggestions that healing was occurring – not least James 5.

I had a slight problem with this view of gifts of healing being given to the sick person and that is they are given in plural to one person. This is a difficult one. It is easily explained if we accept that the gifts are given to the healer and not the healed: the view is that the gifts are given to the healer as and when the Holy Spirit decides and not for all time. As I explained above, I believe, however, the gifts are to the healed. Perhaps there is a solution.

On the cross there is a connection between healing from sickness and salvation from sin, as we have seen. We are given the gift of salvation by God, nobody else can possibly give us salvation or save us, so nobody else can heal us, only God. Now, in a way our salvation is continuous but in a very real sense it is one act, one gift. You can only be born again once. In general use, we understand salvation to primarily mean saving from spiritual death; while healing we understand to mean saving from physical (or mental) pain or death. In the Bible, the word *sozo* is used for saving from sin and for healing from disease (although not in 1 Corinthians 12). There is therefore a very close connection between the two. But if physical healing was one gift like salvation, that would mean we would never physically die which was certainly not true for the Corinthians and is not true for us, unless Jesus comes first. At our new birth, we are saved from the consequence of our sin, once and for ever. God heals us from illness many times in our lives, whether this is through natural means, medical care or miracles. This is why gifts of healing are plural; a gift of healing is given for each illness according to God's will.

Also in illness a number of things might have to be healed. For example, heart disease or stomach ulceration might be caused by stress and anger against colleagues. The stress would make regular time with God difficult. In healing, the heart or ulcer would be healed; the anger against colleagues resolved or healed; and the broken relationship with God restored. We must never forget that when we get better from any illness, ultimately it is God who has healed us. Ambroise Paré, the great French surgeon of the sixteenth century, had a favourite saying: 'I apply the dressing but God heals the wound.'

A permanent calling or an isolated gift?

In 1 Corinthians 12, the expression 'gifts of healing' occurs twice more in the New International Version. In verse 28 we have, 'in the church God has appointed first of all apostles ... also those having gifts of healing etc.' and in verse 30, 'Do all have gifts of healing?' The King James Version has an interesting, if in English an awkward, step. I think it is true to the Greek however. We read: 'and God hath set some in the church, first apostles, secondarily prophets, thirdly teachers, (/) after that miracles, then gifts of healings, helps, governments, diversities of tongues.' I understand the passage to mean that God has set in the church individuals who are apostles, prophets or teachers and in addition to this basic structure he gives miracles, healings, helps or service rendered, governments (literally, steering or piloting), and tongues, when the occasion demands. In other words, once an apostle, always an apostle; once a prophet (or preacher of God's Word), always a prophet; once a teacher, always a teacher; but not always a miracle worker; not always a receiver of healing; indeed not always a helper and so on. Sometimes it is good that someone who is always helping, sits back and lets others do the work. Any Christian may be enabled, on occasion, by the Holy Spirit and given the gift to be a miracle worker, a helper, an organiser, a speaker in tongues, although I believe that the Spirit will also use natural talents. For example, a church minister should primarily be a prophet (preacher) or teacher, but he may also be called upon to do administration. Peter was an apostle but sometimes he worked miracles or was involved in administration. What I am saying is that the first part of the sentence up to (/) is gifts of people and the second part is gifts of things that people do or have.

Called to be healed

The logical extension of what I have written is that any Christian who is seriously ill may be called upon to be miraculously healed. We remember that the gift of such healing will only be given if it is for the common good, building up the church for service, to the glory of God. The person who receives a truly miraculous healing has, in fact, a very heavy responsibility. To the world at large, he or she is a curiosity and for other Christians, it would be so easy to put him or her on a pedestal. The Devil could exploit this by raising feelings of envy. Diana Priest wrote a helpful article: 'Miraculous Healing! – Blessing or Blight?'[3] on this matter. I personally was disappointed when after my operation, the function of my remaining kidney was not completely normal. I am grateful to a Christian friend for pointing out that it is easier for me to deal with other people who are ill, if my illness did not go completely smoothly. Perhaps this is why we hear of many minor things being healed, but not many cases of inoperable cancer or multiple sclerosis. Does this put a different reflection on the, at first, seemingly cruel statement that it may not be God's will to heal? His love is perfect, he does not make mistakes.

I may say, then, miraculous healing may occur if it will build up the church, and if it is not too great a challenge or test for the sick one. What justification have I to write this, from the Word of God? Paul was given his thorn in the flesh to stop him becoming conceited (2 Cor. 12:7). Presumably he was not healed because the temptation to be big-headed would have been too great a test for him. God has promised not to allow temptation or testing greater than we can bear (1 Cor. 10:13). We read of at least two people being healed who after the healing had to bear a great deal of trouble. The man born blind, and healed by Jesus, had to suffer a very nasty inquisition by the Pharisees (John 9:13-34). He was excommunicated but was accepted by the Lord. Lazarus, the man raised from the dead, was a figure of curiosity and his new life was threatened by the Pharisees (John 12:10). Imagine the crowds who would come and stare at him. Many people believed in Jesus because of him. Tradition is that his tomb was a place of pilgrimage in the fourth century. Jesus actually appeared to seek out certain people so that he could heal them as a witness (e.g. John 5:1-16, Matthew 12:9-14, John 9:1-41, and Luke 13:10-17). With Lazarus, Jesus delayed going to help him for four days, until he was well and truly dead. He told his disciples he was glad he was not with Lazarus when he was still alive, so that they would believe when they saw the great miracle (John 11:14). I think I am therefore justified in stating that healing should not be too great a burden for the sick one to bear.

Differing versions
The rendering of 1 Corinthians 12:28-30 is quite different in the various Bible versions as the tables show:

Table 1 – comparing versions of 1 Corinthians 12:28

KJV	RSV	NEB	LIVING	GNB	NIV
God hath set some in the church ... gifts of healing	has appointed healers	those who have gifts of	those who have the gift of healing	those who are given power ... to heal	those having gifts of healing

I believe the correct interpretation of verse 28 is that of the King James Version. It is also interesting to look at more recent versions.

Table 2 – newer versions of 1 Corinthians 12:28

NKJV	NJB	NRSV	REB	NCV	CEV
1982	1985	1989	1989	1993	1995
God has	then	then	those who	those who	he chose
appointed	gifts	gifts of	have gifts	have gifts	some to
... apostles	of	healing	of healing	of healing	... heal
... then	healing				the sick
gifts of					
healings					

The New King James Version, the New Jerusalem Bible and the New Revised Standard Version all agree with the Authorised Version. The, to me, slightly misleading translations of the New International Version and New English Bible are followed by the Revised English Bible and the New Century Version. The Contemporary English Version is similar to the Good News Bible. Word for word translation is: 'And whom set God in the church first apostles, second prophets, third teachers, then miracles, then gifts of healings, helps etc.'[4]

God has given to the church, apostles, prophets and teachers, and he gives gifts of healings to members of the church according to his will. Not every member will receive a gift of healing on every occasion of illness. Some versions do not agree with this interpretation, but to give a different meaning their translators have had to include words that are not actually in the Greek. The New English Bible (and Revised English Bible), New International Version, Living Bible and New Century add 'those who have' to 'gifts of healing', presumably to make the sentence read better. But this subtly changes the meaning. The Revised Standard Version (but, note, not the New Revised Standard Version) uses the word 'healers', the Good News Bible has 'those given power to heal', whilst the Contemporary English Version has 'chosen to heal' which is the same thing. The actual words in the text for 'gifts of healing' are the same as in verse 9.

Table 3 – comparing versions of 1 Corinthians 12:30

KJV	RSV	NEB	LIVING	GNB	NIV
Have all	Do all	Have all	can	not	do all
the gifts	possess	gifts of	everyone	everyone	have
of	gifts of	healing?	heal the	has the	gifts of
healings?	healing?		sick?	power	healing?
				to heal	

Table 4 – newer versions of 1 Corinthians 12:30

NKJV	NJB	NRSV	REB	NCV	CEV
1982	1985	1989	1989	1993	Not
Do all	Do all	Do all	Do all	Not all	every
have	have	possess	have	have	one can
gifts of	gifts of	gifts of	gifts of	gifts of	heal the
healings?	healing?	healing?	healing?	healing	sick

From the tables, it is apparent that there is more agreement over verse 30, except that the GNB has a paraphrase, 'not everyone has the power to heal disease.' The CEV is similar. The Living Bible has: 'Can everyone heal the sick?' I contend that no-one has the power to heal disease, only God. This is exactly the point that Jesus made when he healed the man who was let down through the roof (Luke 5:17-26). Only God can forgive sins and only God can heal disease. The RSV and NRSV have, 'Do all possess gifts of healing?' I do not think this is quite right because it suggests the gifts are owned by someone. The meaning, then, is 'is every sick person healed, given a gift of healing?' The Greek words used for 'gifts of healing' mean the completed act, a cure, which is what the sick person receives direct from God.

Not everybody is healed. We should not despise those who are not.

The answer to the question, in 1 Corinthians 12:30: 'do all have gifts of healing?' is 'no', because the question is also asked, 'are all apostles?' (verse 29). We know from experience that this is true, it is not always God's will to heal the body. At first, I did not think this fits in with the analogy of the church as a body earlier in chapter 12; but it does! Paul says we should not despise parts of the body that are not so attractive or impressive. We should not despise those Christians who are ill and not healed. It is very easy to despise somebody who is mentally ill and pity for the person in a wheelchair can easily be turned into a feeling of superiority. If you do not believe me, ask yourselves why we find it so easy to talk over the head of someone in a wheelchair? We must remember, too, that in a body if one part suffers the whole body suffers. So it is in the body of Christ, the church. Not all are cured and the others must be ready to love and accept the sick person. The others also share the suffering. I have the feeling that this statement may be very profound. I certainly do not understand its depths. At least, it means the others should give of their time to those who are ill. Jesus commands us to love one another, not just in words but in actions (James 2:14-17), even to the extent of laying down our lives for each other, as he did (1 John 3:16-20). Many devoted people have given up their lives to care for another; in the sense of giving up a career or not marrying. Perhaps they do understand what it means to share suffering.

The gift of Faith and the gift of Healing

I have gone into the above in great detail. I have done so because there are three things that are very important when we consider the ministry of healing. These are: the prayer in faith; the gift of faith, which leads to the prayer; and the gifts of healing, which lead from the prayer. As I considered these things I was worried that the above meaning of 'gifts of healing' is different to most commentaries. However, I am glad to note that at least one writer, David Prior, agrees that it is the gifts of healing and not of healers.[5] He states that there are no grounds in the Bible for saying that someone has the gift of being able to heal. Why is it so important? Because saying that healing (and not the power to heal) is the gift, fits in so nicely with James 5. Let's join the two passages:

'And the prayer offered by the gift of faith will bring the gift of a cure from the Holy Spirit to heal the sick person.'

That's wonderful, isn't it? How great it is that parts of God's Word fit together so well. The gift of faith is given to the elders, but the gift of healing is given to the sick one.

No person has a gift of being able to heal, just as the greatest preacher in the world cannot save anybody. But God uses people to heal just as he uses people to save. It is our love, our words, our touch, our prayers, our presence and our comfort that he uses with his love and mighty power to bring healing in its widest sense. Sometimes the gift will be the cure of a serious or chronic disease, but always the gift will be of peace in God's will and so saving the person from bitterness, anger, and sadness.

Wisdom, Knowledge and Faith

The other three gifts I mentioned are also implied by James. They are wisdom, knowledge and faith. When we approach the sick person, how important it is to be wise. Although spiritual gifts can be over and above our natural talents, it is interesting how often wisdom is given to the elderly. In our churches we need to be careful that we do not neglect, at our peril, the advice of our older members as well as the young.

The sick person may have all sorts of misconceptions about their illness or may harbour resentment against their family, their doctor or their God. He may have guilt over something long in his past. We need wisdom as we talk to the sick. Often we need to be quiet and let them do the talking. We need to listen to hear exactly what they are saying, instead of half-listening and deciding what we have to say next. As usual, James gives us the right advice: 'Everyone should be quick to listen, (and) slow to speak' (James 1:19). Perhaps he was thinking of the proverb: 'he who answers before listening – that is his folly and his shame' (Prov. 18:13).

A very common trap to fall into is to tell the sick about our sicknesses, this is rarely helpful. I wonder too about the advisability of telling the sick one of someone else being miraculously healed. There may be a time for this, but certainly not if he or she is feeling far from God due to fear or even guilt. They need to know the love of God first. What is the most important thing about prayer? It is to know that our heavenly Father is listening. Jesus calls us to follow him and to listen to the hurts and fears of the sick one. This takes wisdom and is, I believe, a gift of the Spirit. Many quiet, unassuming people have this gift and we, in the churches, need to find them.

What about knowledge? We have already thought about this in regard to the prayer of faith. The Holy Spirit gives us knowledge about the person, about any hidden fears. He also will give us the knowledge if the person is to be miraculously healed. We see this in the account of the crippled man in Lystra. Paul saw that he had faith to be healed. How did he see? The Holy Spirit gave Paul the knowledge (Acts 14:9). Following closely on knowledge is faith. Faith depends on knowledge. Faith is a gift from the Holy Spirit. Again we remind ourselves that the faith is given to the elders.

I believe that if God wills that a person is healed, we see these gifts working together in the group of elders. To one is given wisdom, perhaps one of the group should converse with the sick one while the others listen. It's difficult for somebody who is ill to talk to more than one person. To another is given knowledge as he listens. This will need to be shared. Then another may be given faith to pray for healing and he will need to encourage the others. Then in God's will, the gift of healing will be given. But wait! Through the group of elders praying, the sick one receives wisdom: he receives the assurance that his heavenly Father loves and cares for him. He receives knowledge to know the future is secure whether his illness gets better or not. He receives faith to remove doubts and fears. No wonder the term is *gifts* of healings and not one gift.

Healing services

Finally, we come to healing services. I used to believe these were wrong because of the emotional impact. We all know that the mind can have powerful effects on relieving symptoms. This can be good and helpful if the sickness is healed but devastating if the symptoms return. Excitement is built up as the date of a healing service to be led by a famous name approaches. The 'healing' occurs perhaps with laying on of hands, perhaps even with 'slaying in the Spirit'.[6] It has happened that later the symptoms return. The person is told that it is their faith on test. They are told they are still healed although their symptoms are still present. I do not believe the Lord would be so cruel. Healing, of course, is often gradual, whether through natural, medical or spiritual means. All I am saying is emotion can be very important in some highly charged circumstances – we need to be careful.

The evidence is, however, that God does heal using healing services. I think there are useful safeguards:

Safeguards for healing services

1. We should not build up men as having the gift of healing, i.e. of being able to cure. Famous evangelists cannot save and neither can they cure. God will and does use men in healing and he uses some men more. They are just like any other Christian. Elijah, we are told, was just like us but great things happened through his prayer (James 5:17).

2. Times for prayer for healing should be part of the normal worship services. I understand that Churches have included it in the Eucharist or Lord's Supper. There is long standing tradition in the Baptist Church for prayer for the sick and needy to be made at the Breaking of Bread. As we meet together to remember our Lord Jesus we are more in unity than at any other time. Because we are thinking of him, selfish thoughts have no part. It seems to me good to offer prayer for healing at the Lord's Table.

3. We should avoid language that will stir up excitement (until after the healing!). It is very much in fashion to imagine the disease. What I mean is that the speaker will use picture language to help the audience and the sick one imagine cancer cells being destroyed. This is usually drawn out in great detail. The technique is called 'visualisation.' I am sympathetic to Livesey's view that Christians should be wary of visualization.[7] He contends that it may open the door to the occult. I must say I was very uncomfortable when I heard it in a healing service. Techniques such as visualization have very little evidence of effectiveness or scientific basis.

Quench not the Spirit

Although I have criticised some healing services, the Holy Spirit will work in his way and according to the will of the Father. We must be careful not to quench him. Paul also said, 'do not treat prophecies with contempt, test everything. Hold on to the good' (1 Thess. 5:19-21). As healing, as well as prophecy, is a gift of the Spirit, I think we can say: do not treat healings with contempt, investigate everything and hold on to the good. This surely is the right advice to a doctor when a patient announces a miraculous healing. It takes a fine degree of wisdom (a gift of the Spirit?) to rejoice with the patient and not to disillusion him, and yet to be ready to pick up the pieces if the symptoms return. This is the approach of Rex Gardner.[8]

If some Christians are helped by emotional, exciting experiences, what does it matter? The danger is that they will travel from meeting to meeting seeking highs, having their weekly 'fixes' instead of maturing in their faith. Then when terminal illness does come, their faith will be strained. The Corinthians were seeking experiences instead of obeying God, and Paul called them infants in Christ unable to take solid food (1 Cor. 3:2).

This book is concerned mainly with serious illnesses so the elders will need to go to the sick person. However, if he is well enough to go to the church service, I think he could because using the gifts that the Spirit gives will benefit the whole church. Great care and wisdom is needed, however, in such a public situation. I feel that most prayer for healing should be in a private situation, as James directed, so that no-one is inhibited and also no-one is over-enthusiastic. Medical consultations are in private because of their sensitive nature, and I cannot see any difference here except that there is a group of elders in contrast to one doctor. James' approach, inspired by the Holy Spirit, is very wise and will completely refute the charges of emotionalism, hysteria or even hypnosis levelled at healing meetings. Of course, when the Lord gloriously answers prayer, this can be made widely known, with the permission of the sick one. This will include those many situations where although the illness is still present, the sick one has had a deep experience of God and is at peace looking at his Saviour.

'Every good and perfect gift is from above, coming down from the Father of the heavenly lights' (James 1:17).

References

1. Cockburn G.T., Department of Classics and Ancient History, University of Durham, personal communication, 1996.

2. Watson D., p.89, *One in the Spirit*, Hodder and Stoughton, 1973.

3. Priest D., 'Miraculous Healing – Blessing or Blight?' in *The Christian Counsellor*' vol. 1, 2:38, 1991.

4. 1 Corinthians 12:28. *The NKJV Greek English Interlinear New Testament*. Farstad A.L., Hodges Z.C., Moss C.M., Picirilli R.E., and Pickering W.N. (Translators) Thomas Nelson 1994.

5. Prior D., p.204, *The Message of 1 Corinthians*, IVP, 1985.

6. 'Slaying in the Spirit' is the term used for the occurrence of collapsing to the floor during the laying on of hands. This happens quite commonly and is not voluntary. I understand it is associated with warm feelings of love. It is claimed to be the work of the Spirit but it is very difficult to

find Biblical justification for this. There are psychological explanations. Francis MacNutt prefers the term 'resting in the Spirit' (*The Power to Heal*, p. 220, Ave Maria Press, 1977). He said that it was a state in which it is more likely than usual that a person will receive healing. Dr Patrick Dixon defined the experience as an altered state of consciousness that is more open to the working of the Holy Spirit (*Signs of Revival*, p. 258, Kingsway, 1994.). He is very positive about it. There is still argument about some of the manifestations but again it depends on the fruit.

7. Livesey R., p.188, *More Understanding Alternative Medicine*, New Wine Press, 1988.

8. Gardner R., *Healing Miracles*, Darton, Longman & Todd, 1986.

Chapter 10

ILLNESS OF THE MIND

Is anyone of you sick? He should call the elders of the church.

Is anyone of you sick in mind – mentally ill? He should call the elders of the church. But what if he does not know he is sick? How then can he call? As I said in chapter two, people with psychological illness are special. This is because they often do not know they are ill. A person with an illness of the mind can be very ill indeed, but he or she may think they are absolutely well and full of energy. Of course eventually they will collapse but that might be too late. Such severe illness is called psychotic illness.

Often the relatives of a person with psychotic illness will ask the church for prayer. This may in fact make the patient worse, even suicidal or at least very angry. What are the elders to do? To think about this, we need to understand a little about mental illness. This is the reason for this chapter.

What are disorders of the mind? First of all, in the vast majority of cases, they are not demon possession. That is not to say that interest in the occult cannot cause mental illness. It can, and interest in the occult is very dangerous. I believe horoscopes, tarot cards, Ouija boards and the like should be shunned.

Psychotic illness

Psychotic illnesses include organic brain disease, schizophrenia, manic-depressive disorder.

Organic brain disease means that there is some physical cause for the mental illness such as infection, drugs, a stroke or possibly a brain tumour. A simple urine infection can cause confusion in old people. Alzheimer's disease, one form of usually senile dementia, is an organic brain disease.

Schizophrenia can be a very frightening illness. Sufferers may think they are somebody else; they may think that rays are affecting them and they may hear voices telling them to do things. They suffer delusions (disorders of thought) and hallucinations (disorders of perception: seeing and hearing). The delusions tend to relate to things that are important in the person's life. Christians may suffer from schizophrenia, just as they may suffer from appendicitis, and because their beliefs are so important, the delusions have a religious content. There is no evidence at all that religion causes the illness. Sadly, because of the bizarre nature of the illness, other Christians have sometimes thought that sufferers are demon possessed.

Manic-depressive disorder has two extremes. On one side is mania or hypomania where sufferers are convinced they have never been so healthy, talk incessantly and rush around trying to do a hundred things at once. If obstructed they may become violent. On the other side is depression where the sufferer is withdrawn, feels hopeless and feels he or she is better off dead.

When Christians become depressed, the worst symptom is often a feeling of unworthiness and rejection by God. This, of course, is not true. When they become manic, they may rush around trying to convert others or may see demons in everybody. It can be readily seen that young Christians can easily be deceived into thinking that the problems or excitement are spiritual in origin.

Psychotic disease, treatment and the church

As I said, people with psychosis do not know they are ill and so can be difficult to treat. Even those with psychotic depression do not accept they are ill, they think their world really is black and hopeless and it is pointless to seek help because nothing can be done. 'A man's spirit sustains him in sickness, but a crushed spirit who can bear?' (Prov. 18:14). For Christians this can be very painful because they may think they have offended God and that he has deserted them. 'Depression is a prison in which the person is both the suffering prisoner and the cruel jailer.'[1] These people do not send for the elders of the church to pray, because either they do not think they are ill; or they feel they are beyond hope. I am glad to say that modern treatment can help.

I think the role of the church in such serious illness is to support once the condition is being treated; to pray in secret; and to be ready to follow James' instructions when the sick one is clear enough to ask. Pfeifer states that uncondemning acceptance by Christians is of great help to people after a nervous breakdown or a stay in hospital.[2] In this way, the sick one will experience love and acceptance in spite of past rejection and their present limitations. When they are improving, and so gaining insight, is the time to suggest they might ask the elders for prayer. Then, also, is the time to mention Biblical verses of God's love. I have quoted Rowe's statement that depression is a prison, this reminds me of Wesley's great words, adapted a little:

> Long my imprisoned spirit lay
> Fast bound in sick depression's night;
> Thine eye diffused a quickening ray,
> I woke the dungeon flamed with light;
> My chains fell off, my mind was free;
> I rose, went forth, and followed thee.

Demon possession

Some people with what appears to be psychotic illness may have demon possession. Virkler described the symptoms and signs:[3]

Physical signs are: increased strength, change in facial demeanour – usually to intense hatred, deeper and harsher voice, epileptiform convulsions and anaesthesia to pain.

Psychological signs are: clairvoyance, telepathy, prediction of future, speaking in foreign tongues, clouding of consciousness and amnesia.

Spiritual changes are change in moral character, extreme

opposition to prayer and inability to say Jesus' name reverently or to affirm that he is God's Son in the flesh.

Obviously some of these things do occur in mental disease but in demon possession they are real, such as foreign tongues and telepathy. I must add that 99.999% of epilepsy is not demon possession but a physical problem of the brain. It is also noteworthy that speaking in tongues may not be of the Holy Spirit.

I have seen many people with severe psychoses, but I have not seen anyone with demon possession. If demon possession is seriously suspected, then I do not think there will be any harm in seeing what the reaction is to the name of the Lord Jesus. The person with schizophrenia may take it up and go on a rambling talk about religion with bizarre expressions, but the person with true demon possession will react very dramatically. I must emphasise, however, that if demon possession is suspected experienced help should be sought. If no experienced help is available, then the safest course is to seek psychiatric help. Psychiatric care will contain the situation until things become clearer. It will also give time to wait on the Lord in prayer. This is a time for wrestling in prayer and so allow the Holy Spirit to confirm or deny our initial impression of demon possession. In this country psychiatric care will initially be found through a General Practitioner. Professor Sims, a Christian psychiatrist, made a very important point about demon possession.[4] He said that somebody who is a true child of God, relying on the Lord Jesus for salvation and therefore being indwelt by the Holy Spirit, cannot be demon possessed (John 14:15-31). So if a Christian starts behaving oddly or even says that the devil is planting thoughts in his head to control him, the treatment will be psychiatric.

Christians can, however, be attacked by Satan and I believe mental as well as physical diseases can be caused by him to try and spoil our trust in God. Treatment will be just as successful as when devils are not involved – we may never know. This may be one explanation why Jesus cured people by casting out demons when to our minds they had conditions that could be treated by modern medicine. Examples of this are the woman who was bent double (Luke 13:10-17) and possibly the boy with epilepsy (Mark 9:14-29, but see below).

There has been mutual suspicion between psychiatrists and certain Christian groups. This is especially so in the care of psychotic illness: demon possession needing deliverance or an organic disease of the brain needing medication. Psychiatrists, with good reason, say attempted and failed exorcism in psychotic disease is very dangerous. But is this not exactly what Jesus said? The disciples were unable to expel the demon in the boy who had fits. Jesus did, but said it was very difficult.

I cannot do justice to this very important subject. I thank God that others already have! I cannot recommend highly enough the book by the Christian psychiatrist, Dr Samuel Pfeifer: *Supporting the Weak – Christian Counselling and Contemporary Psychiatry*, and the chapter on demon possession by Professor Andrew Sims in *Medicine and the Bible*. Barrier's chapter 5 on praying for the sick in *The Kingdom and the Power* is also very useful.[5]

Neurotic disorders or Personality Problems

Does any one of you know that he is sick, but does not realise that the sickness is of the mind, not of the body? How can he ask the elders to pray for him, when they do not know what to pray about? They may suspect what is wrong, but do not know what to do about it. This happens quite often in less serious illness of the mind. The sufferer unconsciously converts the mental symptoms into body or somatic symptoms. This condition, called conversion disorder or somatization, is closely related to anxiety-depression. The anxiety and depression are masked. Sufferers are quite unaware of this and do think there is something seriously wrong with their bodies. They are not malingerers, they do not make up the symptoms. Treatment depends on taking the symptoms seriously and ruling out physical disease. The patient is then gradually helped to realise the true nature of the problem. The underlying difficulty is in expressing emotion, so emotional problems of anxiety or depression are expressed as physical complaints such as chest or abdominal pains.

It is very easy to blame such people for their own troubles but John Wesley castigated doctors for not spotting this condition.[6] He asked why doctors did not consider that bodily symptoms could be caused by the mind? He answered himself by saying that they (the doctors) did not know God. As a doctor I would say that, by his grace, I do know God, but it is still very difficult!

Anxiety/depression, also called neurosis and sometimes a personality problem, is much commoner than psychosis and the sufferer always knows something is wrong. Unfortunately in these conditions there is often shame attached, and for the Christian, deeper shame because he or she thinks, or sadly is often told, that Christians should not get depressed, should not take tablets. In fact, it is more and more apparent that these conditions have their roots in childhood. Parents have awesome responsibilities as well as great joy.

There is a spectrum of disease in depression: at one end is the severe psychotic depression mentioned above and at the other the sad or melancholic personality. In between are all shades of depression, with or without anxiety.

The realisation that one is a guilty sinner needing a Saviour is not a depression. Such a realisation is healthy and desirable if it leads to repentance and surrender to Jesus; while depression is definitely not healthy. Medical treatment and spiritual help are complementary not exclusive. In a Christian sufferer, there is probably no difference between spiritual depression and ordinary depression. The depressed Christian will be treated successfully by a non-Christian psychiatrist; but he will also need the help of his minister or fellow believers. This is exactly the same as a Christian, say, with pneumonia having antibiotics and the prayers of the saints. The person under conviction of sin may appear depressed but he will not get better with the best psychiatric help alone, he needs assurance of sins forgiven and peace with God through the Lord Jesus Christ.

One explanation for anxiety

There is an interesting humanistic explanation for anxiety.[7] Anxiety develops, according to this view, because we never seem to be able to be as good as we should be. This of course is exactly the experience of Paul: 'for what I do is not the good I want to do; no, the evil I do not want to do – this I keep on doing' (Rom. 7:19). This then leads to worry. Paul goes on: 'What a wretched man I am! Who will rescue me....' (verse 24). He immediately answers himself, 'Thanks be to God – through Jesus Christ our Lord!' To the Christian anxiety is transformed! A Christian is not a self-righteous goody goody; a Christian is someone who knows he is a sinner, has asked God for forgiveness and is wholly trusting on the Lord Jesus for this forgiveness. In this life we can never be as good as we should be, but because God loves us and the Lord Jesus died for us, it does not matter! Of course, it goes without saying that because we love our heavenly Father, we try our best to please him. There have been many arguments over Romans 7; some say that up to the triumphant announcement in verse 25 it is Paul's experience before he became a Christian; and others say it is the experience of every Christian struggling with sin in their lives. Some add that it is solved by the Second Blessing or baptism of the Holy Spirit. May I offer a suggestion? These verses are talking about anxiety because of our unworthiness. Paul is showing us that because of the Christian's relationship with God, there is no need to worry: 'There is now no condemnation for those who are in Christ Jesus' (Rom. 8:1). Why? Because the Spirit of life has set us free from our natures which are weak, anxious and, yes, sinful. We still sin, we still are anxious, but we are accepted by God, not condemned. The passage goes on to promise that even our bodies subject to illness and disease (mortal) will have a new life (Rom. 8:11). No wonder Paul shouted, 'Thanks be to God.'

Anxiety/depression, treatment and the church

Because chronic anxiety and depression is often to do with personality, it is difficult to remove completely. Christians can help a lot by providing love and comfort and understanding. When James wrote 'Is any one sick?', I am sure he meant weakness from personality problems as well as physical illness. I think people with these conditions should be encouraged to ask the church for prayer. After all we are all neurotic to some extent, we all have 'hang-ups' of one sort or another, we all are sometimes 'down in the dumps'. Dr. Martyn Lloyd-Jones in his great book on spiritual depression gave the advice to get to know yourself, recognise your own limitations.[8]

There is scientific evidence that 'a life of faith reduces and disrupts neuroses, while a positive piety leads to the healing of such disorders'.[9] Active church membership is protective against illness, but to be fair this is not limited to the Christian Faith.[10]

Low self-esteem

One of the problems for people with psychological illness is that it is far more respectable to have a physical complaint. Patients have said to me that because they look so well, other people are not very understanding.

It is possible that these illnesses are caused, in early life, by a lack of love, and by being ignored. Sometimes, there is a story of more obvious abuse. However, chronic anxiety can develop when the home conditions seem to be very loving. Some of our personality is inherited.

The person with chronic anxiety often has a very low opinion of himself and feels he cannot do anything right – this is called a low self esteem.

The Bible gives very good advice on these matters. The greatest commandment is to love God with all your heart. The second commandment is to love others as much as we love ourselves. We sometimes forget that this means we can love ourselves as much as we love others. Christianity emphasises each person's individual importance to God and as I realise that he loves me, even me, he directs me to serve him and others. Ellison writes: 'The key to positive self-esteem on a daily basis is to act with God's purposes and evaluation in mind. Such an orientation of servant-hood (Col. 3:17-23) frees a person from much of the anxiety and damage of social comparison and negative comments by others.... The inner satisfaction of God's approval becomes a stable source of self-worth.'[11]

Assertiveness and self-esteem

One of the problems people with neuroses often have is the inability to stick up for themselves. They often get 'walked over'. Psychologists try to help this by assertiveness training. The client is taught, by group therapy, to disagree; to defend himself against unfairness; to be able to say 'no' and to ask for help if needed. In so doing, they try to build up the client's self-esteem. This is a good thing but in so doing, other people may be hurt, if the 'sticking up for yourself' goes too far.

A Christian starts from a much more secure foundation. The believer in the Lord Jesus Christ is 'accepted in the Beloved' (Eph. 1:6, AV). We have been chosen by God (verse 4); we have been adopted by him (verse 5). Because of this nobody can remove us from his care (John 10:29). His concern is so great that even the hairs of our head are numbered (Luke 12:7). Our names are written in a Book of Life (Phil. 4:3). The self-esteem of the Christian is based on grace, on unmerited favour. 'By the grace of God,' says Paul, 'I am what I am' (1 Cor. 15:10). This is why we, as Christians, do not need to assert ourselves; this is why we can turn the other cheek; why we can walk the extra mile. We can even consider others' needs greater than our own, because our most basic needs have been met in Jesus. I do not pretend that these things are not difficult!

Our minds guarded by the peace of God

The Bible tells us not to worry, not to be anxious about anything. This seems to be a tall order if we are suffering from an anxiety neurosis. Do you want to have relief from anxiety? Do you want your mind guarded by the peace of God? Do you want your heart set at rest in his presence?

What the Bible says about anxiety and depression[12]

1. *Put God first in your life.* 'Do not worry. Seek first his kingdom and his righteousness.' 'Set your heart on things above, where Christ is seated at the right hand of God. Set your mind on things above, not on earthly things.' 'Humble yourself before God.'

2. *Accept that God loves you, even you.* 'And the peace of God which transcends all understanding will guard your hearts and your minds in Christ Jesus.' 'Therefore as God's chosen people holy and dearly loved, clothe yourselves with compassion, kindness, humility, gentleness and patience.' 'Cast all your anxiety on him because he cares for you.'

3. *Think deeply about good things – meditate about God's goodness.* 'Set your mind (think) on things above.' 'Whatever is true, whatever is noble, whatever is right, whatever is pure, whatever is lovely, whatever is admirable – if anything is excellent or praiseworthy think about such things.'

4. *Rejoice and be glad. Praise God for what he has done.* 'Rejoice in the Lord always. I will say it again, rejoice.'

5. *Allow the Holy Spirit to work in your life. Repent and get rid of things that grieve him.* 'Live by the Spirit, and you will not gratify the desires of the sinful nature. The acts of the sinful nature are sexual immorality .... hatred, discord, jealousy, fits of rage, selfish ambition, envy etc. But the fruit of the Spirit is love, joy, peace, patience, kindness, goodness, faithfulness, gentleness and self-control.' 'Abstain from sinful desires which war against your soul.'

6. *Help other people.* 'Let your gentleness be evident to all.' 'Clothe yourselves with compassion, kindness, humility, gentleness and patience.' 'Let us not love with words or tongue but with actions and in truth. This then is how we know that we belong to the truth, and how we set our hearts at rest in his presence whenever our hearts condemn us. For God is greater than our hearts, and he knows everything.' In other words, if we do our best to help other people in love, even if we think we are no good and unworthy, then God will reassure us.

7. *If you have a problem bring it to Jesus.* 'Come to me all you who are weary and burdened and I will give you rest.'

8. *Be ready to follow him.* 'Take my yoke upon you and learn from me for I am gentle and humble in heart and you will find rest for your souls [minds(?)]. For my yoke is easy and my burden is light.' What is his burden? Surely it is love. He replaces our burden of anxiety, sadness and depression with a burden that is so easy it is not a burden at all. A burden of love, we love him and love others.

Forgive others – inner healing?

Forgiving others is advice given in the Bible, but it is so important that I have given it a section of its own. Jesus emphasised the forgiveness of others to the extent that we should forgive over and over again (Matt. 18:22). Forgiveness is not easy, it is strange how satisfying, yet damaging, it is to nurse a grievance against somebody. Why is forgiveness so important? Why did Jesus emphasise it so much?

Jesus said we are to forgive others because we have been forgiven, and if we will not forgive we cannot expect God to forgive us (Mark 11:25, 26). If we do not forgive we allow Satan to spoil our Christian lives (2 Cor. 2:10, 11).

Paul advises us to bear with one another and forgive whatever grievances we may have against one another. Love binds every-thing together in perfect unity. This allows peace to reign in our hearts in the Lord Jesus (Col. 3:13-15).

The alternatives to forgiving are bitterness, rage, anger, brawling or loud quarrelling, and malice. May I emphasise the bitterness when we cannot forgive? These things, that is the absence of forgiveness, will grieve the Holy Spirit, will sadden him, will hurt him (Eph. 4:30-32). But if we forgive, we are imitators of God (Eph. 5:1).

What does grieve the Holy Spirit mean? He will not leave us because the above passage in Ephesians emphasises that he seals us for ever. The seal of the great God cannot be broken. If we do grieve him we will lose our joy. The Holy Spirit confirms to us that we are children of God and joint heirs with Christ. Adoption is a fact that cannot change. But the experience of this relationship includes our feelings. By him we can cry out with great emotion, 'Father' (Rom. 8:15-17). If we grieve the Spirit, we lose this wonderful feeling of security. If we grieve the Spirit, we will not be filled by him and so have no power to witness. If we are not filled by him we will not bring forth his fruit. The first three fruits that we lose are love, joy and peace (Gal. 5:22).

I don't want to be negative, so let's be positive. These passages teach us that if we forgive those who have wronged us, we will be imitators of God. The Holy Spirit will pour out his love in our hearts (Rom. 5:5), confirming we are God's beloved children, making us cry out with delight, 'Father', as we recognise the working of God in our lives. Love, joy and peace will be our experience. Is this not so? No wonder Jesus emphasised the importance of forgiving others.

There is emphasis today of 'inner healing', also called the 'healing of memories'. The idea is that problems in our minds, such as chronic anxiety, are caused by the suppression of painful memories from the past. These awful experiences are usually suffering caused by others. The counsellor brings these memories out in the open and then prays for the healing of Jesus.[13] There are doubts of the validity of this technique, but most exponents do emphasise the forgiveness of the person who caused the suffering. As far as I go along with it at the moment, I think the important, biblical and effective principle in all this is forgiveness of the bad person through the strength that Christ gives. Bringing such a deep hurt to Christ and so forgiving is healing – these passages confirm it.

Our forgiveness

Chapter 13 in Lloyd-Jones book, *Spiritual Depression*, is entitled 'That One Sin'. He said that a very common problem he had to deal with was Christians whose joy and witness was spoiled by regrets over one great past sin. He answered this problem by pointing to the example of Paul (1 Tim. 1:16) who, despite being a blasphemer, a persecutor and a violent man, was forgiven. If a man who killed the followers of Christ was forgiven, then there is hope for anyone, it does not matter what they have done. Lloyd-Jones went on to say, if we cannot accept that our sins have been forgiven and blotted out, then our problem is *unbelief.*

An important reference on this is found in Acts 13:39. In proclaiming the good news about Jesus, Paul said forgiveness of sins is obtained through him. Paul went on: 'everyone who believes in him (Jesus) is set free (or justified, NIV) from all the sins from which the law of Moses could not set you free' (GNB). This is absolutely wonderful. If I cannot forgive myself for some deed done by me in the past; if the very thought of it makes me cringe in shame, then in a sense I am bound by the memory. I may become depressed and so be prevented from being an effective Christian. Of course, it is the work of Satan. The Lord's glorious answer, if we believe in Jesus, is whatever that sin was, we are set free from it. This is a fact, believe it. Instead of trying to forgive ourselves, we hide in our Lord Jesus.

Jesus the Healer of the mind

I am sure that Jesus dealt with people who had disorders of the mind. We read: 'Jesus went ... teaching, preaching, and healing every disease (*nosos*) and sickness (*malakia*).... and people brought to him all who were ill with various diseases (*nosos*), those suffering severe pain, the demon-possessed, those having seizures (literally, lunatic), and the paralysed, and he healed them' (Matt. 4:23-24). 'And in that same hour he cured many of their infirmities (weaknesses, *asthenes*) and plagues and of evil spirits; and unto many that were blind he gave sight' (Luke 7:21).

We have come across *asthenes* (weaknesses) before and accepted that it included mental as well as physical problems. *Malakia* means weakness, infirmity, softness or misfortune. This would include mental weakness and neurosis. *Nosos* means more serious disease, but it also means to be mad about something, doting on something, raving (1 Tim. 6:4); so surely means raving due to mental illness, i.e. mania. 'Having seizures' or 'lunatic' at first seems contradictory. The belief in those days was that the moon (luna) was the cause of epilepsy and madness. The important point is that Jesus distinguished between demon possession and disease whether mental or physical and he cured them all.

Let us put our trust in him 'who is able to do immeasurably more than all we ask or imagine, according to his power that is at work within us, to him be glory in the church and in Christ Jesus throughout all generations, for ever and ever!' (Eph. 3:20, 21).

God is greater than all our anxieties

There is a Biblical statement that is, without exception, the most perfect assurance to a person with a disease of the mind. I have already quoted it, but it is so important, so lovely that I will quote it again, 1 John 3:18-20:

> Dear children, let us not love with words or tongue but with actions and in truth. This then is how we know we belong to the truth, and

how we set our hearts at rest in his presence whenever our hearts condemn us. For God is greater than our hearts and he knows everything.

This is perfect for a Christian with a serious psychotic illness because all it asks is that we help other people according to the truth that we have, or according to the ability that we have. I believe that the most seriously disturbed Christian with schizophrenia is obeying this verse if he does the smallest kindness for a fellow-sufferer. The Christian with depression can be helped by being reminded of even small kindnesses to others when he or she feels unworthy. When we see what 'heart' means in the Bible, I think you will agree with me. It means mind, understanding, will, memory, intention and conscience.[15] Just replace 'heart' with each of these words in turn in the above passage and see what I mean. 'Mind' speaks of all psychological illness; 'understanding' reminds me of schizophrenia; 'will' of the lack of motivation in depression; 'memory' of organic brain diseases like dementia, Alzheimer's; 'intention' of extreme shyness or low self-esteem; and 'conscience' of those nagging doubts in many diseases including obsessional/compulsive disorder.

I mentioned above that we should know ourselves. So much psychological illness is in our natures. We may have to accept residual schizophrenic symptoms; we may have to accept compulsive thoughts; we may have to accept a melancholy nature. William Cowper suffered greatly from depression all his life but what great hymns he wrote.

God moves in a mysterious way,
his wonders to perform;
he plants his footsteps in the sea,
and rides upon the storm.

You fearful saints, fresh courage take;
the clouds you so much dread
are big with mercy, and shall break
in blessings on your head.

'And the God of all grace, who called you to his eternal glory in Christ, after you have suffered a little while, will himself restore you and make you strong, firm and steadfast' (1 Peter 5:10).

In conclusion, serious illness of the mind is very frightening and confusing. Expert psychiatric help should be sought, accompanied by prayer in secret. When the person is improving, he is welcomed in love, simple prayer is offered in the name of the Lord with the repeated assurance that Jesus loves him. The same principle of love applies to those with less serious illness.

References

1. Rowe D., *Depression. The way out of your prison*, Routledge and Kegan Paul, 1983.

2. Pfeifer S., p.194., *Supporting the Weak*, Word Publishing, 1994.

3. Virkler H.A., 'Demonic Influence and Psychopathology' in *Encyclopaedia of Psychology*, p.297, Ed. Benner D.G., Baker Book House/ Marshall Pickering, 1985.

4. Sims A.C.P., 'Demon Possession: Medical Perspective' in *Medicine and the Bible*, Ed. Palmer B., Christian Medical Fellowship, Paternoster Press, 1986.

5. Barrier R., p.219, *The Kingdom and the Power*, ed. Greig G.S. & Springer K.N., Regal Books, 1993.

6. p.165, in *John Wesley's Journal*, abr. by P.L.Parker, Hodder and Stoughton, 1993.

7. Holmes D.S., p.110, *Abnormal Psychology*, Harper Collins, 1994.

8. Lloyd-Jones D.M., *Spiritual Depression*, pp.16,17, Pickering Paperbacks, 1965.

9. Hark H. (GER.), quoted in Pfeifer S., p.96, *Supporting the Weak*.

10. Hannay D.R., 'Religion and health', Soc. Sci. Med.14,(A),6835, quoted in Markus A.C. et. al., p.92, *Psychological Problems in General Practice*, Oxford University Press, 1989.

11. Ellison C.W., 'Self-Esteem', p.1047 in *Encyclopedia of Psychology*.

12. I have mixed the references up. They are: Matthew 6:25-34; Matthew 11:28-30; Galatians 5:16-26; Philippians 4:4-9; Colossians 3:1-17; 1 Peter 2:11; 5:6,7; 1 John 3:11-20.

13. Taylor H., Chapter 8, 'Inner Healing' in *Sent to Heal. The Order of St. Luke the Physician*, Australia, 1993.

14. Lloyd-Jones, *op. cit.* p.65.

15. Zodhiates S., p.1701, '2588 – *kardia*' in *Hebrew-Greek Study Bible*, Eyre & Spottiswoode, AMG, 1984.

Chapter 11

A TROUBLED MIND AND A SICK BODY

*Is any one of you in trouble? He should pray. Is anyone
happy? Let him sing songs of praise. Is any one of you sick?
He should call the elders of the church* (James 5:13).

'Is any one of you sick?' Is it possible that he is sick with a physical
disease, but the disease is caused by psychological problems?
The illness could be cured by medical means, covered by the
prayer of the elders, but the sick one is not completely healed
because the psychological problems remain. It has long been
thought that mental stress or a certain personality could cause
physical disease. For example, a very common assertion in some
Christian books, for example, is that a bitter, unforgiving character
is often the cause of rheumatoid arthritis. I think such a sweeping
statement is very unfair. One of my loveliest patients has very
severe rheumatoid arthritis. Indeed sitting here, I cannot think of
one of my patients with arthritis who is very bitter. Sadly, I can
think of many bitter people who have not got arthritis! However, I
think we do need to consider this subject which is called
psychosomatic illness.

Five diseases were thought to be psychosomatic, that is caused
by the mind: high blood pressure, heart disease, rheumatoid
arthritis, stomach ulceration and ulcerative colitis. Some also
included cancer. If it is true that bitterness, anger or fear cause
physical illness, then it is possible that if the bitterness, anger or
fear are healed, the physical illness might get better. There is little
evidence that this is so except perhaps in heart disease, but books
are still being published which say that it is. This causes
unnecessary suffering.

Holistic Medicine

There is a great deal of talk today about holistic medicine. But it is very important that treatments directed at the whole person should be supported by, or at least not contradicted by, scientific medicine and must not include anti-Christian ideas. So much of New Age ideology is superficially attractive but is ultimately anti-Christian. Holistic care is not new. But as we have seen, in using the term 'save' for healing, James meant healing of the whole person. A person is not completely healed or whole until he is united with his God through the Lord Jesus who is the only Way to the Father.

Holistic medicine means treating the whole person: in biblical terms, body, soul and spirit. Illness affects the whole person – illness is holistic! Cancer of the lung caused by smoking may affect the mind (or soul) by fear and the spirit by anger against God. However, that is very different from saying that fear or anger cause cancer of the lung, and that removing the fear or anger will cause the cancer to get better. Such extreme psychosomatism implies that the mind and body are against each other.

The Nature of Man

In the Bible, man is a unity of body, soul and spirit. The words for soul and spirit often seem to be used interchangeably, especially in the Old Testament. The basic word in the Hebrew is the word that is usually translated as 'soul'. 'Soul' means the living being, for example: 'the LORD God formed the man.....and the man became a living being (soul)' (Gen. 2:7). The soul is the inner self, the real 'me' as opposed to the outer appearance.

The New Testament uses three words to describe man. They are body (*soma*), soul (*psyche*) and spirit (*pneuma*). Body, soul and spirit are a trinity. I cannot escape the conclusion that this is similar to the other Trinity. Does being made in the image and likeness of God mean I am a trinity as God is a Trinity (Gen. 1:26)? We could parallel it in this way. God the Father is the Will;

my mind is my will. Jesus is the One who does God's will; my body does what I will. The Holy Spirit, who also does God's will, is especially thought of as fellowship or contact with God; my spirit responds to that contact. The Godhead is total unity. So are we, unless part of us is missing. If the spirit is missing or dead, the unity is lost, the harmony of mind and body is disturbed and illness is possible.

The Bible suggests that in those who do not know the Lord Jesus as Saviour and Lord (i.e. the unregenerate), the spirit is dead. Such a person, according to the Bible, is incapable of responding to God. This is why Jesus told us we must be born again. Belief in the Lord Jesus Christ, becoming a Christian, being saved, includes being born again in the spirit. This new life of the spirit restores the harmony of the three in one. There is then the possibility of freedom from disharmony or disease, and this actually will be realised when our bodies are raised imperishable (1 Cor. 15:42).

Paul, in commenting on the resurrection, produced an interesting insight. He wrote in 1 Corinthians 15:44 that the body before death is a natural body (*psyche soma*) and that at the resurrection it will be a spiritual body (*pneuma soma*). Jesus' resurrection body is capable of amazing things, but he still ate (Luke 24:39, 43), so his body is still physical, although it is spiritual. Our physical bodies, at present, are governed by our natural minds and are subject to disease. The mind-body unit or psyche-soma is indivisible before death, so disease, whatever the cause, affects the whole. Illness of the body affects the mind and illness of the mind affects the body. Disease affects us and the effects vary in mind and body depending on the disease. The mind may not cause a physical disease but it can modify it. Demoralisation and depression are common reactions to physical illness, but there is no evidence that they are the cause of the illness.[1] This is why I think it is so important and lovely that James emphasises the raising of the sufferer up to look at the Saviour in spirit.

Is there any evidence that mental disorder or upset causes

physical illness? Before considering some medical evidence, does the Bible shed any light on it?

The Bible and psychosomatism

In Psalm 38 we read: 'There is no soundness in my flesh because of your anger. Nor any health in my bones because of my sin .... My wounds fester and are loathsome because of my sinful folly .... My back is filled with searing pain, there is no health in my body' (verses 3, 5, 7). Psalm 38 suggests that physical and mental distress can be caused by God's punishment for sin, or at least by the believer's guilt over sin.

Psalm 41:1-3 has: 'Blessed is he who has regard for the weak .... The LORD will sustain him on his sickbed and restore him from his bed of illness.'

The advice in Proverbs 3:7 and 8 is: 'Fear the LORD and shun evil. This will bring health to your body and nourishment to your bones.'

I do not believe that God is the author of illness, but sometimes God does send illness to bring us to our senses. But good men and women who help the weak (cf. Psalm 41) also get sick. The Psalms, especially, were written when the author(s) were in deep distress, crying out to God. Guilt and shame can easily attribute the suffering to an angry God. These passages do suggest at least that guilt and shame can cause physical as well as mental illness.

Medical Knowledge

There is slowly increasing evidence that the mind, or its reaction to stress, can cause physical disease. At the moment, it is far from proven. The most convincing evidence is in heart disease.

There is a personality type that has been associated with heart disease – personality type A. Type A individuals tend to be more competitive, concerned with achievement, aggressive, hostile, over-committed and driven by a sense of urgency. A hostile nature seems to be the most important. There are, of course, other things associated with heart disease such as age, weight, cholesterol, high blood pressure and smoking. But it seems that, when these things are allowed for, men who easily become angry, irritable or 'gripe a lot' are more likely to have heart disease. No wonder that God said: 'It is mine to avenge; I will repay' (Rom. 12:19); and, 'Do not let the sun go down while you are still angry' (Eph. 5:26). As Jesus showed, it is not wrong or harmful to be angry when anger is needed. It is wrong and probably harmful to persist in anger, yet it is also harmful to suppress anger if it is needed. There are many nice, patient people who also have heart disease.

Again, it is possible that a person inherits the liability to be easily angered as well as a liability to heart disease. If that is the case, anger and heart disease would be related, but one would not cause the other. More recent research has cast doubt on the association between type A personality and heart disease, but other research has shown that if a person who has had a heart attack modifies his behaviour, he is less likely to have another. Suppression of anger is as bad as losing your temper all the time. It depends on the situation.

It is possible that worry, stress, severe disappointments or a hostile nature may cause physical disease. James gives us good advice: if we are in trouble we should pray, rather than getting angry; and if happy sing songs of praise, rather than rejoicing in our own cleverness or achievement which is usually at the expense of others. Jesus encouraged us to learn from him, he is gentle and humble, so that we would find rest for our souls [minds] (Matt. 11:29).

Cancer and the mind

For many years people have said that depression has been associated with the development of cancer. Researchers have looked back at cancer sufferers' lives and they have reported depression. It is all too easy for people with cancer, and sad because of it, to look back and say they were unhappy in the past. However, a few studies have looked forward and reported an increased incidence of cancer in people who were depressed at the time the study started.

Some other researchers have claimed that a certain personality is associated with cancer. It is interesting that it appears to be a direct opposite to the type A personality of some people with heart disease. Not surprisingly it is called the type C personality. I must emphasise that not all people with cancer have this personality, it is just a trend that some researchers have noticed.

A German author, Bammer, found certain characteristics associated with cancer patients.[2] His characteristics are: courtesy and cordiality, submission to authority, submission to social norms, ready neglect of one's own feelings, sense of responsibility, conscientiousness and zeal, religiosity, altruism and sense of sacrifice, inhibition of aggressive feelings, guilt, readiness to be self-critical, feeling of inferiority and depressive tendency. I was concerned when I read this as some of these features are encouraged or even commanded in Scripture.

More research is needed on this and so far the evidence is conflicting. Below is a comparison of Bammer's characteristics with the Bible's teaching. Cancer risk personality traits (after Bammer) are followed by the Biblical teaching (in italics):

1. 'Courtesy and cordiality.'
Do not think of yourself more highly than you ought (Rom. 12:3).
    Be completely humble and gentle (Eph. 4:2).
    Let your gentleness be evident to all (Phil. 4:5).
    Clothe yourselves with compassion, kindness, humility, gentleness and patience (Col. 3:12).

2. 'Submission to authority.'
Blessed are the meek, for they will inherit the earth (Matt. 5:5).
    Show true humility towards all men (Titus 3:2).
    Submit yourselves for the Lord's sake to every authority instituted among men (1 Peter 2:13).

3. 'Submission to social norms', (following the herd).
Live as free men....Show proper respect to everyone (1 Peter 2:16,17).

Stand firm then, with the belt of truth buckled around your waist (Eph. 6:14).

4. 'Neglect of one's own feelings, behaving according to what others expect.'

If someone strikes you on the right cheek, turn to him the other also. If someone wants to take your tunic, let him have your cloak also. If someone forces you to go one mile, go with him two miles (Matt. 5:39-41).

Honour one another above yourselves (Rom. 12:10).

5. 'Sense of responsibility, conscientiousness and zeal.'
Be like minded [like Christ who made himself nothing] *(Phil. 2:2).*

You were called to suffer for doing good ... because Christ suffered for you leaving you an example that you should follow in his steps. When they hurled their insults at him, he did not retaliate, when he suffered he made no threats (1 Peter 2:20,21).

Do not merely listen to the word .... Do what it says .... Pure and faultless religion is to look after orphans and widows in their distress and to keep oneself from being polluted by the world (James 1:22,27).

6. 'Religiosity.'
But seek first his kingdom and his righteousness (Matt. 6:33).
I want to know Christ (Phil. 3:10).

7. 'Altruism and sense of sacrifice.'
If anyone would come after me, he must deny himself and take up his cross and follow me, for whoever wants to save his life will lose it but whoever loses his life for me will find it (Matt. 16:24).

8. 'Inhibition of aggressive feelings.'
Love your enemies and pray for those who persecute you (Matt. 5:44).
Bless those who persecute you (Rom. 12:14).

9. 'Guilt, readiness to be self-critical, feeling of inferiority and depressive tendency.'

Therefore there is now no condemnation for those who are in Christ Jesus, because through Christ Jesus the law of the Spirit of life set me free from the law of sin and death (Rom. 8:1, 2).

If we endure, we will also reign with him (2 Tim. 2:12)

... heirs of God and co-heirs with Christ, if indeed we share in his sufferings in order that we may share in his glory (Rom. 8:17).

In his great mercy he has given us new birth into a living hope .... who through faith are shielded by God's power .... In this you greatly rejoice, though ... you may have had to suffer grief in all kinds of trials (1 Peter 1:3-6).

If Bammer's nine traits are a true picture of the personality of a person with cancer, and it is by no means certain they are, they are certainly not a true picture of the Christian. The Christian is in a perfectly secure position because of the love and grace of God. Trait 9 does not apply to the child of God at all. The other traits do describe Christians to some extent, but as the Bible quotations show, the Christian has those characteristics from a position of strength. The Christian is meek, but will inherit the earth; the Christian is submissive, but is free and stands firm for the truth; the Christian allows others to use him, but by so doing is imitating the Lord Jesus; the Christian is religious, but everything is promised by God; the Christian does deny himself, but in so doing will have a more satisfying life; the Christian does inhibit aggressive feelings, but in so doing attempts to win his enemy for Christ.

I think it is clear to see that although the Christian life is full of self-denial and putting other people first, suffering is consecrated to God by the example of Christ. Many Christians have experienced suffering, catching leprosy, TB, and plague because of their self-denial. Paul, talking about his suffering, said: 'I fill up in my flesh what is still lacking in regard to Christ's afflictions for the sake of his body which is the church (Col. 1:24). The Roman Catholic

Church especially has put suffering, including illness, on a higher level by emphasising this verse.

It is possible that stress, reaction to stress, or other psychological problems, may cause physical as well as mental disease. At present it is unproven. It is certain, however, that not all (and probably only a very little of) illness is caused by stress, just as not all illness is caused by sin. It is not in our power to cure ourselves from most illnesses by reducing stress and thinking healthy thoughts full of courage and love.[3] Those who say that we can are wrong and are certainly not teaching biblical truth.

I don't see how we can ever know that disappointment or stress, in the individual patient, is the cause of disease. If personality or reaction to stress cause disease, then we are responsible for our own diseases. Somebody with cancer will look back to see what caused the problem. This will make it difficult for them to trust that the heavenly Father has everything under control. Instead of looking back, we should look forward and ask his help in our present condition, even if we have a serious illness. 'And we know that all things work together for good to them that love God, to them who are called according to his purpose' (Rom. 8:28, AV). What is his purpose? For us to be conformed to the likeness of his Son, so that we may be in the family of God and brought to glory. Let us praise him, who loves us so much.

Let us suppose, then, that the sick one has a physical disease caused by reaction to stress or a personal attribute. He should still ask the elders for prayer, and rest in the love of God. He can leave the worries about what ultimately caused his sickness to God. We are advised to pray about everything, with thanksgiving and without anxiety, because the Lord is near. His peace, which is beyond understanding, will guard our hearts and minds in Jesus (Phil. 4:5-7). Cast all your anxiety, even what caused your illness, on God because he cares for you' (1 Peter 5:7).

Life in God's Service

I have already mentioned that heart disease may partly be caused by an aggressive, hostile personality or by being too involved in the 'rat race'. If this is the case, and the sick one cannot see it himself, this is one time where a Christian friend can gently point it out in love. If this does fall to the elders, they would need to be very careful and gentle. Most importantly, they should wait on the Lord for wisdom. Then James' words would apply, 'if he has sinned, he will be forgiven.' James has wisdom about the 'rat race': where there is envy and selfish ambition, there you find disorder; fights and quarrels come from desires that battle within; selfish desires are unfulfilled (James 3:16; 4:1,2). It is not surprising that high blood pressure and angina happen if there is 'disorder and battles within'.

The advice in the Word of God is: 'Do not conform any longer to the pattern of this world, but be transformed by the renewing of your mind' (Rom. 12:2). This is an ongoing work of the Holy Spirit. The whole of Romans 12 is good advice in this situation; the Good News Bible entitles it, 'Life in God's Service.'

References

1. Gelder M., Gath D.,& Mayou R., p. 410, *Oxford Textbook of Psychiatry*, Oxford University Press, 1989.

2. Bammer K., *Krebs und Psychosomatik*, Stuttgart:Kohlhammer, quoted by Guex P., *An Introduction to Psycho-Oncology*, Routledge, 1994.

3. Sapolsky R.M., pp.160-161, 'Why Zebras don't get Ulcers', W.H.Freeman and Co, 1994.

Chapter 12

I AM READY TO GO HOME NOW

'Is any one of you in trouble? He should pray. Is anyone happy? Let him sing songs of praise. Is any one of you sick? He should call the elders of the church to pray over him and anoint him with oil in the name of the Lord. And the prayer offered in faith will make the sick person well; the Lord will raise him up' (James 5:13-15).

What if the sickness is very severe? After all, the Bible uses the term 'unto death'. What if there is no hope that the sick person will get better? I am thinking, for example, of paraplegia or severe congenital disorders. We have seen that if it is God's will, the faith will be given to save or heal the sick person and he will be raised up. We have also seen that a truly miraculous healing will only be given if it will build up the church; to make the people of God stronger; *and* if it is not too great a burden for the sick one to bear. We know that in any illness or condition, the Lord will bless through the prayer of faith, even if there is not a cure. Bitterness and sadness will be healed; anger will be forgiven; and the Christian will be raised up out of misery. We also know that complete healing and cure will occur after death at the resurrection when there will be a new body. Is the answer, then, to terrible illness, for the Christian to seek death; to take his own life; or to ask others to do it for him?[1] Is healing to be found through euthanasia?

The cure of disease

Naturally, at times of serious illness or injury, the priorities are to alleviate suffering and to cure, if possible. For the Christian this will include seeking God. When serious illness appears, the biblical teaching is to seek medical help and at the same time to ask the church for prayer in order to seek a cure. Yet, because our lives are finite and medical science is imperfect, cure is not always possible.

An alternative to cure?

Serious disease, whether the infectious diseases and trauma of the past or heart disease and cancer of today, is so often fatal. Yet it is not all gloomy, for modern medical treatment is very effective. God has been very gracious in imparting knowledge, and medical advances are really very exciting. Sadly we now also have the problems of chronic wasting disease and various forms of paralysis, where it is possible to keep people alive with modern technology but with severe disability. It is worth looking at the experience of people in the past, where any treatment was so often impossible.

One such set of experiences is the Black Death or plague in the 14th century which can be assessed because there is information available.[2] Between one third and one half of the population in Europe died during the Black Death. There was an awful finality about it: if you became sick you died. There was nothing the church or doctors could do about it. There were two main beliefs: (1) the plague was a punishment sent by God for sin; (2) it was sent by God to hasten the Christian's arrival in heavenly bliss. The response to the first was to repent of sin, seek God's forgiveness through Jesus Christ and prepare for death. The second response was to welcome death as an old friend to attain Glory. The first response also welcomed death as there was then no risk of further sin (in the original sources, the truth of salvation through Christ freeing from the effect of future sin did not seem to be understood).

The argument was, therefore, that as death could not be avoided, it should be welcomed.

The alternative, then, to seeking cure in chronic serious or mortal illness is to accept death or even to seek it. The sick one has so much pain and suffering that surely it would be better to die and then join the Saviour in heaven. Paul had a lot of trouble and pain in his life and he said: 'I desire to depart and be with Christ, which is better by far' (Phil. 1:23). Euthanasia is a plan to make this longed-for death come sooner and easier. James, however, did not say, 'Is any one of you in trouble? Seek death!' What he said was, 'Pray about it'. At its best, euthanasia is the planned agreement by doctors with a sick person to end his life because of intolerable suffering. The obvious danger is abuse by unscrupulous people. Euthanasia as recommended by the Voluntary Euthanasia Society is suicide: the taking of one's own life even though assistance is given by others.

It used to be said that suicide was an unforgivable sin, but there are no grounds for that conclusion in the Bible. To the Christian nothing, not even death nor life, can separate him from his heavenly Father, although I am sure that he is saddened by such an event.

Suicide was well known in ancient times and indeed was admired by the Greeks. It is strange how silent the Bible is about it. I can only conclude from this that suicide does not ultimately affect a person's relationship with God, except that it is too late then for an unbeliever to come to God for salvation.

When suicide is mentioned, the Bible accepts it as a matter of fact. The most famous suicides are King Saul and Judas Iscariot. King Saul was defeated in battle and severely wounded; he did not want to be tortured by his enemies, so he killed himself (1 Sam. 31:1-4). Judas killed himself in remorse when he saw what he had done in betraying Christ (Matt. 27:1-10).

What advice does the Bible give?

James' advice to us is : 'Is any one of you in trouble? He should pray.' The word translated 'in trouble', *kakopatheo*, means to 'suffer evil'. The same word is used for Christians suffering because of their faith (2 Tim. 1:8; 2:3). The word for evil or bad, *kakos*, is used for illness in Matthew 14:35, Mark 1:32, and Luke 7:2. The people in these accounts were ill, they were suffering, literally they were having it bad. If anything awful or evil is happening to us, we should pray about it. If we are suffering, we should pray about it. Our loving heavenly Father invites us to let him share in our suffering. Prayer means letting God into our lives.[3]

Job's story

Job has always been an instructive case for Christians who are in trouble. James mentioned Job as an example of perseverance in the face of suffering (James 5:11). His suffering, including serious illness,[4] seemed to happen to him for no apparent reason. Job's experience, then, is very like the experience of anybody who is suffering due to sickness, when there is no apparent reason for the suffering. Job's reaction to suffering is very interesting and helpful to us. From Job chapter one the reader has an insight into the explanation for Job's suffering, but he did not know it himself, at least at the time of his suffering.

The following are some of the outbursts wrung out of Job by his suffering:

Job 3:11,13,16: 'Why did I not perish at birth, and die as I came from the womb? ... For now I would be lying down in peace; I would be asleep and at rest .... Or why was I not hidden in the ground like a stillborn child, like an infant who never saw the light of day?'

Job 3:20-22: 'Why is life given to those in misery, and life to the bitter of soul, to those who long for death that does not come, who search for it more than hidden treasure, who are filled with gladness and rejoice when they reach the grave?'

Job 3:26: 'I have no peace, no quietness; I have no rest, but only turmoil.'

Job 6:8-10: 'Oh, that I might have my request, that God would grant what I hope for, that God would be willing to crush me, to let loose his hand and cut me off! Then I would still have this consolation – my joy in unrelenting pain – that I had not denied the words of the Holy One.'

Job 6:14,15: 'A despairing man should have the devotion of his friends, even though he forsakes the fear of the Almighty. But my brothers are as undependable as intermittent streams...'

Job 7:4: 'When I lie down I think, "How long before I get up?" The night drags on, and I toss till dawn.'

Job 7:16: 'I despise my life; I would not live for ever. Let me alone; my days have no meaning.'

Job 7:19-21: 'Will you never look away from me...? If I have sinned, what have I done to you, O watcher of men? Why have you made me your target? Have I become a burden to you? Why do you not pardon my offences and forgive my sins?'

Job 9:27,28: 'If I say, "I will forget my complaint, I will change my expression, and smile," I still dread all my sufferings.'

Job 10:1-3,6,20,21: 'I loathe my very life, therefore I will ... speak out in the bitterness of my soul. I will say to God: Does it please you to oppress me ... that you must search out my faults and probe after my sin? ... Turn away from me so that I can have a moment's joy before I go to the place of no return.'

Job 12:4,5: 'Even my friends laugh at me now; they laugh, although I am righteous and blameless; but there was a time when God answered my prayers. You (his friends) have no troubles, and yet you make fun of me; you hit a man who is about to fall.' (GNB)

Job 13:23,24: 'How many wrongs and sins have I committed? Show me my offence and my sin. Why do you hide your face and consider me your enemy?'

Job 19:6,7,21: '... then know that God has wronged me ... Though I cry, 'I've been wronged!' I get no response .... Have pity on me, my friends, have pity, for the hand of God has struck me.'

Job 21:7,9,23-25: 'Why do the wicked live on, growing old and increasing in power? ... Their homes are safe and free from fear .... One man dies in full vigour, completely secure and at ease. Another man dies in bitterness of soul, never having enjoyed anything good. Side by side they lie in the dust.'

Job 31:35: 'Oh, that I had someone to hear me!'

What is Job saying? He wished he had never been born or if he had that he had been exposed outside to die. (This was a very common occurrence in ancient times; equivalent to abortion today – Job was saying he wished he had been aborted!) He wondered why unhappy people had to continue to live. His mind was in turmoil. It would be so much better to die. He was so close to suicide at that point.

Job had the pain of friends deserting him when he was in desperate trouble. At one stage, he decided to pretend to others that everything was alright and yet he knew it wasn't. He tossed and turned all night not finding any rest. Life was pointless. He complained to God why these things were happening to him.

Job was also worried that if he continued to suffer, he would eventually sin against God in his bitterness. So it was safer to die – this is very similar to the medieval people welcoming death so that there would be no further risk of sin. (It is sad that the freedom of Christianity was overlooked; Paul gave thanks to God as he realised this very anxiety in his own unworthiness is covered by the blood of Jesus.)

Job loathed life, so he asked God to leave him be so that he could have a little happiness before he died. He felt that his friends had kicked him when he was down. He felt that God was against him, so he pathetically pleaded for pity from those around him.

Job could not understand that bad people seemed to do well and did not even worry about death. When it came after a long life they seemed to be content with their families around them. Yet, he said, what's the point? Happy men and depressed men all die and rot away, just the same.

Job blamed God, he blamed everybody else. Nobody takes any notice, it's not worth carrying on. Surely suicide is better – end it all. He was right down. Are these words not exactly what we think or say today when we are in trouble? Suffering people are like Job.

Sadly, unremitting trouble in life often leads to bitterness or mental illness or to suicide. How many embittered people comfort themselves in their bitterness? How many people with serious mental disorders have fled from reality? How many of those who have taken their own lives, did so because they could not see the point of continuing to struggle against impossible odds?

Elihu suggested that Job was wishing that he had been selfish and had not cared for others (Job 36:21). If he had lived for himself, perhaps these things might not have happened, and anyway it could not be any worse and he would have had some fun. Do not we sometimes think that? The Christian life can be such a struggle; would it not be easier to look after ourselves and be selfish? This is a very common temptation by the Devil when things are difficult: 'If only I hadn't gone to help so and so, perhaps this illness or accident would not have happened to me.'

Yet in the midst of all this, Job also said:

Job 19:25-27: 'I know that my Redeemer lives, and that in the end he will stand upon the earth. And after my skin has been destroyed, yet in my flesh I will see God; I myself will see him with my own eyes .... How my heart yearns within me.'

Job 13:15: 'Though he slay me, yet will I hope in him.'

Job 23:10: 'He knows the way that I take. When he has tested me, I shall come forth as gold.'

There is much argument over what the passage in Job 19 means. I believe it describes a foretaste of the experience of a Christian.

Even if there is terrible suffering, even if the suffering results in death, God will be there to put it right – will vindicate the sick person. This reminds me of a little boy who was severely handicapped but who was looking forward to heaven because there God would make it up to him. Certainly, the Lord will make it up to those of his children who have suffered. But I do think he can begin now as we trust him.

Job had his wealth and health restored to him, but before this happened God spoke to him. Job's response was: 'My ears have heard of you but now my eyes have seen you' (Job 42:5). James said in regard to Job's perseverance in suffering: 'The Lord is full of compassion and mercy' (James 5:11). God has promised not to try us more than we are able to bear (1 Cor. 10:13). Whatever suffering we have we can rest assured that God has not given up on us. There is always hope. The biblical inference on euthanasia is that God will always comfort and help his child who is suffering; there is, therefore, no cause for despair and no need for suicide or euthanasia.

Christians will suffer illness and pain just like anybody else. The biblical promise is that even in our suffering, God will not leave us. In light of this truth we should pray that if real suffering comes our way, we will be able to praise him. Joni Eareckson Tada has experienced real suffering. She has been almost completely paralysed for a quarter of a century and yet her Christian faith shines through her writings.[5] Paul and his fellow workers' experience was they were hard pressed but not crushed; perplexed but not in despair; down but not out; persecuted but not abandoned. Their bodies were wasting away but inwardly they were renewed each day so they did not lose heart. They felt that in their suffering, they shared in the death of Jesus, so that they had his new life revealed in their weakness (2 Cor. 4:8-10,16).

Depression and suicide

There is a very great and important exception to what I have written about suicide above and that is in psychiatric illness. Suicide in this situation is caused by the disordered thought processes in the illness. Paul reminds us that even death – there is no qualification as to the cause of death – cannot separate us from the love of God that is in Christ Jesus. Indeed I am bold enough to imagine the surprise and delight that a depressed Christian who has taken his own life will receive on arrival in glory. The chains will fall off indeed!

Dear Christian friend, if you have a relative who you were so sure belonged to the Lord Jesus and yet took his own life, rest assured that he is now safe in the arms of his Saviour. Suicide in depression is not a rational act. It is so important in people who are terminally ill not to overlook clinical and therefore treatable depression. In one study of the terminally ill, two out of three people who wanted euthanasia were clinically depressed but only one person in thirteen who did not want to die was depressed.[6] Many of those whose depression was treated then wanted to live.

When a person who is depressed commits suicide, they are, in fact, dying from the illness just as somebody dying from a heart attack dies from the illness.

Relatives ask for euthanasia

In my experience, it is not usually the sick person who asks for euthanasia, it is the relatives. They feel so helpless and sorry that their loved one is suffering that they ask that something is done. The intention in the last hours or days is to make the person comfortable. This may need large doses of drugs.

Good care whether at home, in a hospice, or in hospital is very effective at relieving the symptoms of terminal disease. We don't need to be frightened of large doses of morphine, as addiction does not occur in this situation. A drug similar to morphine can now even be applied as a patch on the skin.

Who owns the body?

A frequent claim by those who advocate active euthanasia or suicide is that the sufferer's body belongs to him alone; therefore he has a right to end his life if he so wishes.[7] The Christian's response to this is, 'Not so.' The bodies of believers are not their own, but are the temples of the Holy Spirit. It is important to remember that this is because they have been bought with a price – the precious blood of the Lord Jesus. Of course, this argument that our bodies are not our own primarily applies to Christians (1 Cor. 6:19,20). There is a real paradox here: the Christian who accepts he does not own his body will receive a new perfect body at the resurrection. Apparent slavery means perfect freedom. I do not know what to write about this to the non-Christian, except to say in love that nothing makes sense outside the family of God. God loves you and wants you as his child, whoever you are.

It seems to me there is nothing wrong in desiring death. Many people slip away sooner than the extent of the disease would suggest. I have seen this in Christians as well as those who seem to have no faith. What is wrong is for other people to actually procure the death.

The Elders

Suppose a Christian with a life threatening illness has called the elders to pray for her. Let's also suppose they are not given the authority by the Holy Spirit to pray the prayer of faith for a miraculous cure. They will, of course, pray according to the faith they have been given. The disease progresses and the Christian is obviously at the end of her life on this earth. One would hope that the medical and nursing care is excellent and the person is comfortable. Incidentally, there is certainly a place for prayer that medication and other palliative treatment will work.

The elders call again and are greeted by the sick Christian who says, 'I am ready now,' or 'I want to go home now,' or something similar. What should their response be? First of all, it is so important not to deny the fact of the impending death. The important thing is to show love and concern – to hold hands, perhaps to embrace and, yes, to weep with the sick one. There is also joy present as the Lord becomes very real. The elders will perhaps anoint again and pray. Perhaps favourite songs will be sung quietly and Bible passages read. The Lord will raise the sick one up, not from the bed, but to see him in spirit and soon to see him in reality.

Let us ask God to help us to be with those in their final journey, to comfort and encourage. Let us be ready to be strengthened and uplifted by the witness of the sick one as to the reality of her faith. We can't avoid being sad but the joy is so much deeper.

Severe disability

In the main, I have been discussing people who are dying anyway. Joni Tada advises those who are severely disabled but not actually dying. The main points I gleaned from her book, there are probably others, are:

don't kill yourself because you have friends who care about you;

don't kill yourself because you would be playing into the hands of the devil;

don't kill yourself because God loves you.

Don't kill yourself because you have friends .... This puts a huge responsibility on the rest of us. But what a privilege! We turn to James: 'Pure and genuine religion is this: to take care of orphans and widows in their suffering and to keep oneself from being corrupted by the world' (James 1:27, GNB). He also advises us to help the poor, and he states that faith without deeds (saying 'God bless you' to someone who is suffering but not helping them materially), is dead (2:26). He also reminds us that we sin if we don't do the good that we know we should do (4:17).

Conclusion

On balance then, active euthanasia is wrong. It is wrong for the unsaved (those who have rejected Christ) because they then lose for ever the opportunity to come to God. I think it is wrong for Christians because of all the arguments above. There is, however, an important practical point which means that no Christian doctor can ever be involved in active euthanasia. This point is that no human, however saintly, can be sure of another's relationship to God.

I would like to conclude by using Joni Tada's insight.[8] Euthanasia is not really an option because however ill we are, we can show God's love to those around us; because our suffering has meaning to God now and forever; and because God is at work in us however weak our bodies are.

References

1. For the person who is not a believer in the Lord Jesus Christ, the answer is 'no', apart from those who cannot reject Christ – by reason of age or maldevelopment of the brain.. However, severe the suffering is, there is always hope that the sick one will come to Christ.
2. Horrox R., *The Black Death*, Manchester University Press, 1994; Rawcliffe C., *Medicine and Society in later Medieval England*, Alan Sutton, 1995.
3. Hallesby O., *Prayer*, IVP, 1993.
4. Job's disease is not known. It certainly made him very ill. Suggestions as to its nature are, boils, ichthyosis, eczema, psoriasis, pemphigus, smallpox or even leprosy. R.B. Zuck suggested that Job's illness was some form of pemphigus. That certainly would fit in with the severity of his disease, but would not fit in with Job scraping himself with a piece of pottery (*The Bible Knowledge Commentary*, Old Testament,'Job', p.721, Ed. Walvoord J.F. and Zuck RB. Victor Books 1985).
5. Eareckson Tada J., *When is it right to die?*, Marshall Pickering, 1993.
6. Cochinou H.M., Wilson K.G., Enns M., Monchun N., Lander S., Levitt M., & Clinch J.J., *Desire for death in the terminally ill*, ' Amer. Jour. Psychiatry, 152:8, 1995, pp.1185-1191.
7. Dworkin R., *Life's Dominion*, Harper Collins, 1993.
8. Eareckson Tada J., *op. cit.* p.118, 119.

Chapter 13

A HEALING MINISTRY

The main reason for writing this book was because I wanted to work out the relevance of my Christian faith to problems of human suffering and illness in my work as a doctor, and in my life as a man. I have been thrilled as, to my mind at least, my studies in God's Word, especially James 5 and 1 Corinthians 12, have confirmed that Christianity is very relevant to my personal experience of sickness and to my day to day care of the sick. I praise God for this. I offer the contents of the book to those who are sick, and to those who care and pray for them.

Health and healing is not the same as cure. A man or woman is not completely healthy, however free they are of disease, unless they are united with God through Christ. Being healthy includes having a good relationship with others and with our surroundings. A person can be healthy or whole before God and yet have a disease which is not cured. Complete healing, freedom from all disease, will only occur in heaven.

In this last chapter, I would like to draw everything together and detail how to go about praying for the sick in our local church fellowships. James said, 'Do not merely listen to the word. Do what it says' (James 1:22).

From the previous chapters, there are a number of points I would like to emphasise:

1. The promises in this passage are for all Christians.

2. The sickness or weakness can be of any kind. Nothing is excluded.

3. The sick person should ask the church for prayer.

4. Illness or sickness hurts the whole church, not just the individual.

5. The Lord Jesus, himself, suffered weakness or sickness, so he has been tempted like us.

6. The elders, representatives of the church, should gather together in unity.

7. Prayer is in the name of the Lord, in faith, in the Spirit.

8. The faith is given to us by God. Sometimes he gives us the faith to pray for a miracle. Sometimes he gives faith to ask that the sick one will be blessed and given peace. At other times he gives faith to ask that the medical treatment will be successful.

9. The prayer in faith will heal or save the depressed, sick person. The Lord will raise him up out of his misery.

10. By faith, given by God, his head will be raised or lifted up out of his distress to experience afresh the love of his Lord Jesus.

11. Miraculous healing will only be given if it will benefit the whole church.

12. Miraculous healing will only be given if it is not too great a challenge, test or burden for the sick one to bear.

13. Not many serious illnesses are healed because this would put too much pressure on the person who is healed.

Additional advice to the sick in mind or body is:

1. Think about other people.

2. Put their needs before yours.

3. Pray for each other continually.

4. Forgive those who have wronged or harmed you.

5. Ask forgiveness from those you have wronged, if any.

6. Accept that because of what Jesus has done, the Almighty God will accept your prayers as your loving heavenly Father.

7. Expect your prayers will be effective.

8. If you are too ill to do this, then rest in his love because he cares for you.

9. If there is a sin in your life, confess it to God and ask his forgiveness, as you forgive others. He will not turn you away.

10. If you are not aware of unconfessed sin in your life or if you have confessed your sin, then forget it. Your Father sees you pure, clothed in the righteousness of his Son.

11. As you believe in the Lord Jesus Christ, you are indwelt by his Spirit; it is impossible for you to be possessed by an evil spirit, whatever others may say.

Message to the sick person

- Is any one of you sick, weary or depressed?
- You should ask the church leaders to pray for you in the name of the Lord, perhaps anointing you with oil.
- The oil will signify your complete dependence on your heavenly Father and submission to his will.
- Prayer, according to the faith that God will give in the Holy Spirit, will bring a gift of healing from the Holy Spirit which will be the perfect gift for you.
- You will be lifted up in spirit and body to see Jesus by faith. His love will pour out in your heart.
- If you need forgiveness of sins, you will freely be forgiven.
- In our church fellowships, let us agree our faults together before God and pray for each other so that we will be healed of guilt and bitterness and healed of sickness if the Lord wills.
- The Lord hears and answers the prayers of his children as they continue to walk in his light.

The invitation is very clear: if you are sick, call the leaders of your church to pray for you. Call your doctor to treat you as you continue to trust in God.

'I sought the LORD, and he answered me; he delivered me from all my fears. Taste and see that the LORD is good' (Psalm 34:4,8).

Message to church leaders

- Encourage the sick to ask you, the servants of the church, to pray for them.
- Do not be anxious about it, but make sure you are in unity, even to the extent of confessing your faults to each other.
- Seek the Lord's will and guidance and then go and pray for the sick in the wisdom, knowledge and faith that God will give you.
- Offer to the sick person anointing with oil. Encourage him in the name of the Lord.

'Taste and see that the LORD is good.' We should not worry that by praying for healing we give the sick false hope. As long as we pray according to the guidance and faith that God will give, we have nothing to fear.

Paul's words to Timothy are apposite in connection with the healing ministry. 'For the Spirit that God has given us does not make us timid; instead, his Spirit fills us with power, love, and self-control' (1 Tim. 1:7, GNB). Healing is in the power of the Spirit. As we walk in love and in his light, he will protect us or, rather, he will protect the sick from our mistakes.

Message to nurses, doctors and other health professionals

- Let us pray to God and ask him to help us to relieve pain and if possible to cure the illness.
- If cure is impossible, let us continue to care and give hope.
- We should not lie to the sick person but should lovingly tell the right amount of truth.
- Let us encourage the sick person to ask the church for prayer.
- Let us be ready to pray with the sick person if he desires.

- We should co-operate with the church, but respect the confidence of our patient.
- While the elders are to pray, we are to treat to the best of our ability.

I pray that God will use this book to help the sick, to build up his people to serve him, and to bring glory to his Holy Name.

'The life I live in the body, [with its pain, disease, disappointment and joy], I live by faith in the Son of God, who loved me and gave himself for me' (Gal. 2:20).

Greek text

I again acknowledge the immense help and fascinating material I found, as a Greek illiterate, in the following works:

The Hebrew-Greek Key Study Bible, Edited by Spiros Zodhiates, Eyre & Spottiswoode/ AMG, 1984.

The NKJV Greek English Interlinear New Testament, Translators, Farstad A.L., Hodges Z.C., Moss C.M., Picirilli R.E., Pickering W.N., Thomas Nelson, 1994.

Vine's Complete Expository Dictionary of Old and New Testament Words, Vine W.E., Unger M.F., White W.Jr., Thomas Nelson, 1985.

Further reading

Atkinson D., *The Message of Job*, IVP, 1991.

Benner D.G., Ed., *Encyclopedia of Psychology*, Baker Book House/ Marshall Pickering, 1985.

Brown M.L., *Israel's Divine Healer*, Paternoster Press, 1995.

Carson H., *Spiritual Gifts for Today?*, Kingsway ,1987

Dudley M., Rowell G. Eds., *The Oil of Gladness*, SPCK, 1993.

Eareckson Tada J., *When is it right to die? Euthanasia on trial*, Marshall Pickering, 1993.

Fergusson A., Ed., *Health: the Strength to be Human*, IVP, 1993.

Frank D., *Tough Questions about Healing*, Highland Books, 1994.

Fyall R., *How God Treats His Friends* (a study of the Book of Job), Christian Focus Publications, 1995.

Gardner R., *Healing Miracles*, Darton Longman & Todd, 1986.

Gelder M., Gath D. and Mayou R., *Oxford Textbook of Psychiatry*, Oxford University Press, 1989.

Greig G.S. and Springer K.N., *The Kingdom and the Power.*

Are Healing and the Spiritual Gifts used by Jesus and the Early Church meant for the Church Today?, Regal Books, 1993.

Guex P. (trans. Goodare H), *An Introduction to Psycho-Oncology*, Routledge, 1994.

Gunstone J., *The Lord is our Healer*, Hodder & Stoughton, 1986.

Harper M., *Jesus the Healer*, Highland, 1986.

Holmes D.S., *Abnormal Psychology*, Harper Collins, 1994.

Howat I., *Pain My Companion*, Christian Focus Publications, 1990.

Howat I., *When the Thornbush Blooms*, Christian Focus Publications, 1992.

Kelly D. F., *If God Already Knows Why Pray?*, Christian Focus Publications Ltd., 1995.

Lloyd-Jones D.M., *Spiritual Depression, its causes and cure*, Pickering Paperbacks, 1965.

Maddocks M., *The Churches Healing Ministry*, SPCK, 1981.

Markus A.C. et. al., *Psychological Problems in General Practice*, Oxford General Practice Series 15, Oxford University Press, 1989.

Palmer B. Ed., *Medicine and the Bible*, Christian Medical Fellowship/The Paternoster Press, 1986.

Pfeifer S., *Supporting the Weak. Christian Counselling and Contemporary Psychiatry*, Nelson Word Ltd, 1994.

Sapolsky R.M., 'Why Zebras don't get Ulcers. A guide to stress, stress-related diseases, and coping', W.H.Freeman and Co., 1994.

Smith A.M., *Gateway to Life*, IVP, 1994.

Steptoe A.& Wardle J., *Psychosocial Processes and Health – a Reader*, Cambridge University Press, 1994.

Taylor H., *Sent to Heal*, The Order of St. Luke the Physician, 1993.

Twycross R. and others, *Mud and Stars*: A report of a working party on the impact of hospice experience on the Church's ministry of healing, Sobell Publications, 1991.

Watson D., *Fear no Evil*, Hodder & Stoughton, 1984.

Watt, Sir James, Ed., *What is wrong with Christian Healing. Churches Council for Health and Healing*, 1993.

White J., *The Masks of Melancholy. A Christian Psychiatrist looks at depression and suicide*, IVP, 1982.

Wimber J. & Springer K., *Power Healing*, Hodder and Stoughton, 1986.

Yancey P., *Where is God when it hurts?* Pickering & Inglis, 1979.

Scripture index

Persons Index

Bible Characters

Subject Index

Dilwyn Price became a Christian during his boyhood in north Wales. Later he studied medicine at Newcastle-upon-Tyne University. In 1980 he settled with his wife, Pam, and their three children at Shotley Bridge, where he combined general practice with part-time hospital surgery. He became a deacon, junior church leader, and occasional preacher at Blackhill Baptist Church. He was a devoted family man, and enjoyed reading, music and fell walking.

Dilwyn began this book in 1994 while convalescing after surgery. In 1996 cancer was diagnosed again, but he continued to prepare his manuscript, completing his work two weeks before his death on 21 November 1996 at the age of 49.